TIMELESS
NORTH AMERICA

Great Parks That Capture Nature's Wonders

Edited by **FRANCESCO PETRETTI**

METRO BOOKS

NEW YORK

Contents

TEXT
FRANCESCO PETRETTI

EDITORIAL DIRECTOR
VALERIA MANFERTO DE FABIANIS

GRAPHIC DESIGNER
MARIA CUCCHI

EDITORIAL STAFF
GIADA FRANCIA
ALESSANDRA PEZZUTTO
MARCELLO LIBRA

*1   FROM LEFT TO RIGHT: GLACIER BAY NATIONAL PARK IN ALASKA, CAYO COCO
IN CUBA AND THE PLATEAUS INSIDE THE GRAND CANYON IN ARIZONA.*

2-3   IN WINTER, SNOW COVERS MONUMENT VALLEY'S PEAKS AND VALLEYS.

4-5   WRANGELL-ST. ELIAS NATIONAL PARK, SEEN FROM ABOVE.

6   THE PEAKS OF BRYCE CANYON ARE WHITENED WITH SNOW.

7 AND 8-9   THE CASTLE MOUNTAIN AND THE TURQUOISE LAKES OF BANFF NATIONAL PARK.

*10-11   IN THE KATMAI NATIONAL PARK, GRIZZLY BEARS GATHER IN THE VICINITY
OF THE RAPIDS WHERE SALMON CAN EASILY BE CAUGHT.*

© 2007 White Star S.p.A.
Via Candido Sassone, 22/24
13100 Vercelli, Italy
www.whitestar.it

This 2008 edition published by Metro Books,
by arrangement with White Star S.p.A.

Translation text: Christina Recchia
Translation captions: Glenn Debattista

Metro Books
122 Fifth Avenue
New York, NY 10011

ISBN-13: 978-1-4351-0626-0
ISBN-10: 1-4351-0626-1

Printed and bound in Indonesia
1 3 5 7 9 10 8 6 4 2

Color separation: Grafotitoli, Milan

Preface

North America

Yellowstone was the world's first national park. It was founded in 1872 during the period when, for American society, the myth for the conquest of the West was still fresh and current. At that time, a powerful element of that nation's society, richer and more active than the mass, was actively transforming a vast, wild territory, devoid of any attractions for most people, into a region subjugated by men and put into the service of a civilization which increasingly consumed natural resources.

Perhaps it was the devastating effect of the massacre of the bison, 60 million animals destroyed in a brief span of a few dozen years and transformed into a cemetery of bones alongside a railroad directed toward the Pacific. Maybe it was the disappearance of the passenger pigeon, the bird that used to darken the skies with thousands of flocks during its migrations. Or perhaps it was the tragic end of native cultures erased by the new and dominant white civilization. In short, the totality of different factors demonstrated to a group of enlightened men that nature had its limits and there was the danger of wiping out; in a short period of time, those landscapes and elements which had been the background and frame for the birth and development of the planet's most prosperous nation.

The establishment of Yellowstone Park was a stepping stone in the history of the movement for the preservation of nature. It showed that only the actual implementation of commitments could safeguard the geysers and the prairies, the torrents rich with salmon, the resin-perfumed woods, the bison herds and the ferocious but fascinating grizzlies. Since 1872, the United States and its large neighbor, Canada, have never interrupted their commitment to the protection of the environment. It can be truly said that today, the biggest and most unitary conservation project in America is represented by national parks system and by the two nations' other protected areas. Overall, these now include all the salient elements of wildlife and of the vast North American continent's natural environment.

Mexico, despite its scarcity of resources and the problems of a less flourishing economy, and also Guatemala, burdened by its population's daily problems, have to some extent carried on in the south their large northern neighbors' conservation mission; they have assured the safety of some of the world's most beautiful tropical areas.

From the realm of the polar bear in the North, to the prairies of the bison, to the deserts of the saguaros and coyotes, to the pine forests of California and the deciduous broad-leafs of Appalachian, to the lush swamps of the Gulf of Mexico, and to the Rocky Mountains' craggy peaks, and ending with lush tropical forests and stormy seas brimming with life, North America presents itself to the visitor as a continent full of variety and fascination, the total sum of all the wonders of the Earth.

The parks, in their varied typology which runs from large wilderness areas to National Parks, natural monuments, and nature reserves, constitute today the most efficient bulwark to prevent what scientists describe as the "sixth extinction." Some 4.5 billion years have passed since the appearance of the first life forms on Earth, or rather, in the oceans, a very long time in which life, not only in animal and vegetable forms, but also in those of microorganisms, has continued to modify, adapting itself to the conditions which gradually were being created on the planet. Multicellular organisms date back to around 540 million years ago and since then, least five times, a mass extinction of vegetable and animal species occurred on the planet.

Some 440 million years ago 25 percent of the life forms which at the time populated the seas became extinct; the worst hit were the trilobites. About 370 million years ago, during the Devonian Period, another massive crisis occurred in the world of the vertebrates and also that of primitive fish, just when the first terrestrial life forms were starting to appear. The Permian Period, 250 million years ago, coincided with the third mass extinction, the most catastrophic of all because of the disappearance of 50 percent of all animal families, among which were the trilobites and several insect species. Then 210 million years ago, during the Triassic Period, as mammals and dinosaurs started to appear, reptiles similar to mammals and several invertebrates disappeared. The fifth extinction, the most recent one, was that of the dinosaurs; it dates back to the Cretaceous Period, 65 million years ago.

These extinctions have a common denominator: natural causes like great geological phenomena and climatic changes or extraterrestrial events like the impact of a meteorite – which plausibly caused the dinosaurs' extinction in the Cretaceous Period. Moreover, these processes of extinction developed and concluded themselves during a long period of time that spanned thousands, even millions, of years.

They certainly did not occur in the span of a few centuries, and the new life forms produced by evolution have gradually filled the emptiness they left. In fact, the disappearance of the dinosaurs paved the way for the development of mammals.

And we now come to the sixth extinction. During the course of the last twenty centuries it is calculated that around 200 species of mammals and birds have ceased to exist, a third of these during the last fifty years. Contrary to the five preceding ones, the still ongoing sixth extinction is caused by man's colonization of the planet; it is the first time in the history of life that the ecological expansion of a single species has exerted such a large influence throughout the entire biosphere.

Man is in direct competition with the other species for every resource; his ecological niche continually expands, constricting that of other life forms. As if that were not enough, man alters and fragments the ecosystems, moves animals and plants from one region to another and thus exacerbates the fight for survival between species which, not having evolved together, have not developed the tools necessary for living together.

Scientists have estimated the dimensions that the planet's ecological occupation have reached. They state that mankind appropriates to itself, or destroys or manipulates 40 percent of the net primary productivity; that is, of all biological productivity which the plant world sets up for the other organisms of the planet.

The World Conservation Union has estimated the extinction threat within species, by the percentage likely to be lost: vascular plants, 12.5 percent; birds,

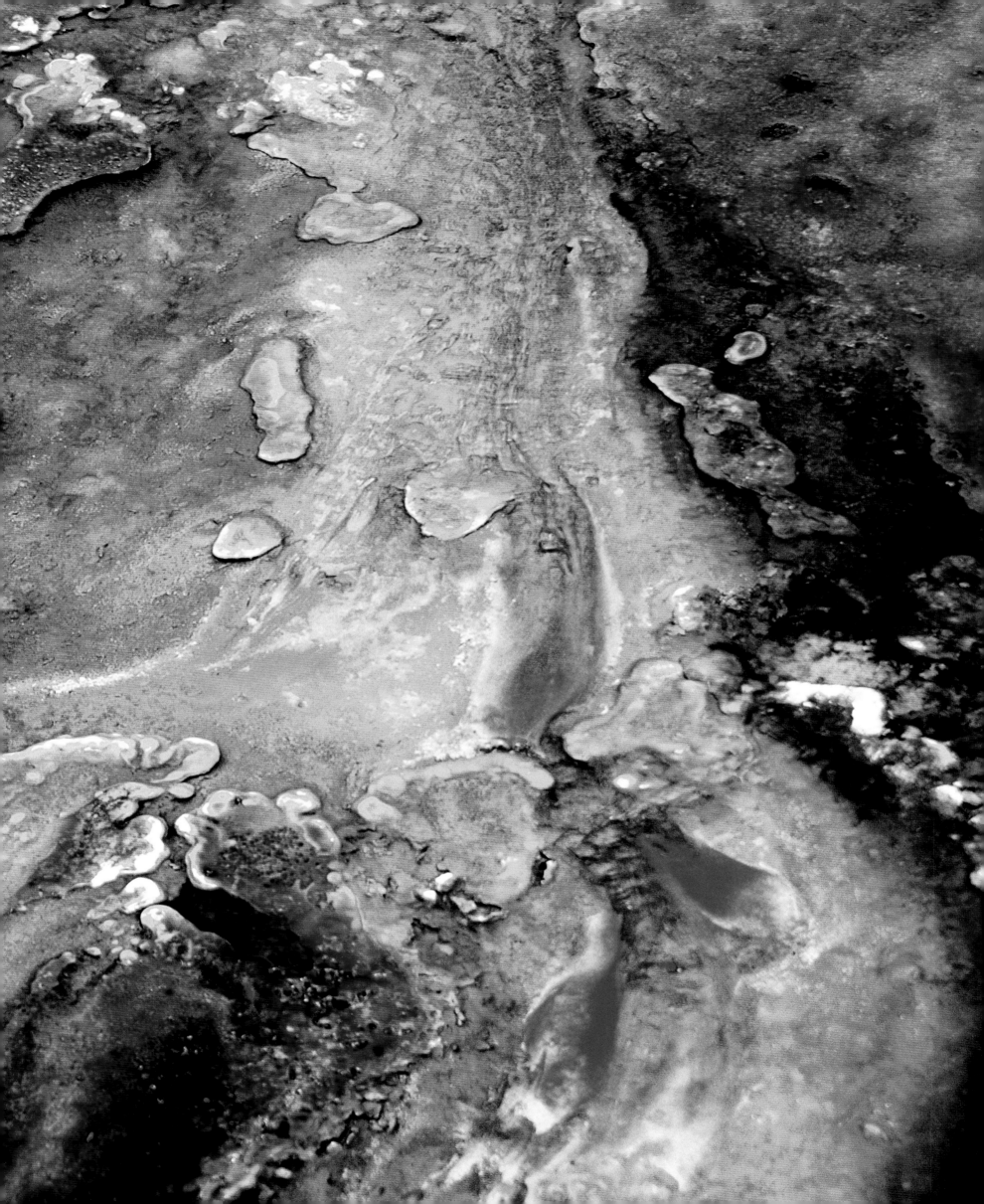

11; reptiles, 20; mammals, 25; amphibians, 25; and fish, 34 percent of 11,00 species. Ornthologist Stuart Pimm offers higher percentages: 50 percent of the planet's flora and fauna could become extinct during the next century.

In contrast to previous extinctions, this one is occurring in the brief span of two centuries, and is in danger of leaving an emptiness which could hardly be replaced even over millions of years. Some 300 species and subspecies of mammals, 400 of birds, 183 of fish, 138 of amphibians and reptiles and various numbers of invertebrates risk disappearance on earth in the brief span of some dozens of years. In some cases, the most urgent action is essential: fewer than 30 California condors, only 5 pairs of Chatham Island robins, fewer than 800 Apennine wolves, no more than 100 night parrots or New Zealand kakapos, and 10 Mauritius kestrels now survive — and that survival hangs by a thread.

Much harder hit by the phenomenon of the sixth extinction are the fauna of recent and explosive human colonization zones, such us North America. This continent has experienced dramatic losses, among them are the passenger pigeon and the great auk, a large sea bird which lived along the North Atlantic coast. Also emblematic is the almost complete extinction of the bison, the great wild ox. At the beginning of the 19th century some 60 millions grazed on the American prairies, only to be ruthlessly hunted down by white settlers.

The future of nature, of plants and animals, of those capable of resisting the offensive of man in natural ecosystems, of those able to find a vital space in manmade environments and of those which will continue to provide food and products for humankind or keep them company in the cities and zoos, depends mostly of a new mentality.

This mentality will have to combine a competent scientist's rationality and the sensibility of a zoophile naturalist. It can be found — it is the mentality that guided the pioneer ecologists at the end of the 19th century when they proposed, to the President of the United States, the institution of a large national park in the Yellowstone region so that the natural heritage considered to be every citizen's legacy would not be lost.

In the American continent enormous resources and the most modern breeding techniques are now used to halt the spread of the sixth extinction. The California condor has been raised in an aviary and then reintroduced in the silent Californian Mountains. Thanks to man, the wolf has returned to pursue deer and bison in Yellowstone National Park.

From this continent, and from its natural paradises, administered competently and wisely with scientific spirit but also with the desire to involve the full range of public opinion, comes a great lesson of civics: parks can thus remain fundamental elements of natural systems, sources of pleasure for those who love to observe them, see images or simply know that resources, to be utilized thriftily, still exist, subjects of scientific researches and conservation projects.

The institution of the protected areas in the American continent, as in the rest of the world, has been determined not only by the necessity for conservation, but, also by opportunities of various types. It is not by chance that the main protected areas of North America are mountainous territories, whose orographic and climatic conditions used to render them of little interest to men, or areas which are only marginal to human activities.

Far fewer, perhaps not so much in number but certainly in area, are the protected areas in flat terrains, valley bottoms, and along watercourses. This situation is common in a majority of the developed countries; they penalize the conservation of such environments.

Nonetheless, the now extensive and linked protected areas guarantee the preservation of the biodiversity of a large and now particpiating geographic region which includes the United States of America, Canada, Mexico, and Guatemala. This volume focuses on the parks that are most representative of the major natural environments, defined by landscapes and by fauna and flora. An array of striking images will assist the reader in exploring these great parks.

15 THE TALLEST TREES IN THE WORLD ARE PROTECTED INSIDE SEQUOIA NATIONAL PARK.

16-17 THE KENNICOTT GLACIER PLUNGES LIKE A GREAT RIVER, CONSTANTLY ERODING THE BARE ROCKY SLOPES.

18-19 THE COLORS OF SPRING INVADE THE VALLEYS OF GLACIER NATIONAL PARK, MONTANA.

20-21 THE BARRIER REEF OF CAYO COCO, CUBA, EXTENDS IN FRONT OF A VERY LONG AND FINE SANDY BEACH.

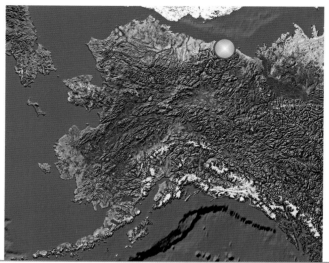

22 TOP LEFT THE SNOWY OWL IS CHARACTERIZED BY ITS WHITE PLUMAGE.

22-23 LARGE HERDS OF CARIBOU CROSS THE TUNDRA AT THE START OF SPRING.

23 TOP LARGE FLOCKS OF SNOW GEESE PREPARE FOR THE LONG FLIGHT AT THE END OF SUMMER.

23 BOTTOM LIFE FLOURISHES IN THE SWAMPS DURING THE SHORT ARCTIC SUMMER.

Arctic National Wildlife Refuge
Alaska

This refuge includes a vast area of coastal tundra and mountain land in almost completely uninhabited northeastern Alaska. In fact, people are found only in small residential areas and primarily work in oil drilling.

Thus the land is left for the full enjoyment of the approximately 200 bird species, at least 45 mammal species that range from the miniscule pygmy shrew to the large right whale. Almost 19.2 million acres (7.7 million hectares) of the protected area is considered "wilderness area" and three rivers that flow through it are called "wild rivers." This means that the three waterways, the Sheenjek, Wind and Ivishak, are left in completely natural states; residents and visitors are forbidden to do anything that might alter the water system or the banks. Roads, except for a rocky-bottomed stretch of Dalton Highway, are completely absent and moving from place to place is done by small plane.

The movements and the cycles of expansion and contraction of the glaciers have strongly influenced the territory of the park in recent millennia, creating a varied and tormented landscape in which deep, rocky canyons alternate with vast marshes and steep heights, their sides cut out by glaciers. Today, part of the area still offers food resources to the Inupiaq (Eskimo) community located along the coasts, who hunt ocean mammals, and to the Athabasca Indian tribe in the area more inland.

The flora and fauna of the park are of the arctic and subarctic type, with a few species of great interest to both the scientist and the visitor who ventures into this area. Three species of bear live here: the polar bear, the grizzly (or brown) bear, and the black or baribal bear. There is also a significant population of herbivores, in particular caribou, Dall sheep, the musk ox, and moose that are the prey not only of the bear but also of wolves, wolverines (a powerful predator) and lynxes.

In the coastal zone there are killer whales, attracted here by the concentration of salmon, whales, sea lions, sea otters and thousands of ocean birds of the gull and tern, the guillemot and puffin, and other species. During the migration season flocks of snow geese and wild ducks crowd the muddy banks along the coast and the ponds to feed.

23

25 TOP THE CARIBOU REACH SUMMER
GRAZING STILL COVERED
IN SNOW. THEY RELIEVE THEIR
HUNGER, BY EATING THE SPARSE GRASS
AND THE LICHENS THAT SPROUT
FROM THE ICY TERRAIN.

25 BOTTOM RISING SPRING
TEMPERATURES CAUSE THE GRADUAL
BREAKUP OF THE ICEPACK, AND
THE "LIBERATED" WATER
BECOMES ACCESSIBLE.

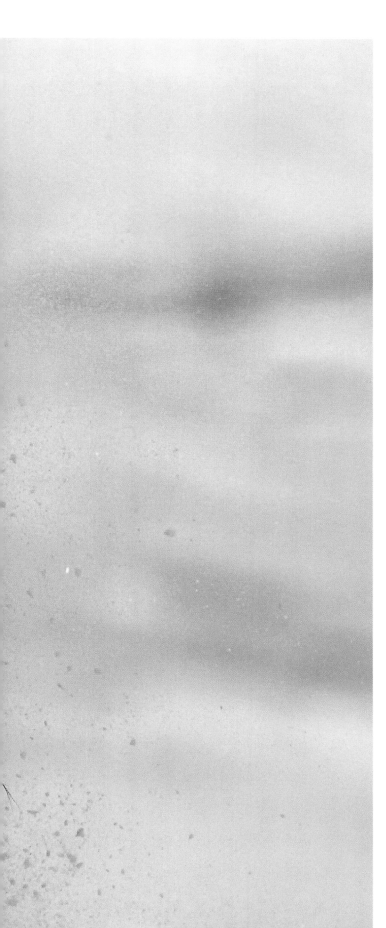

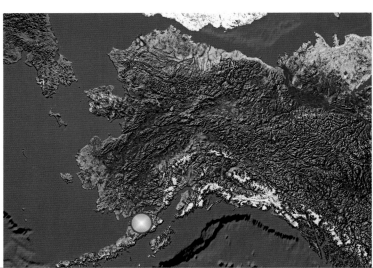

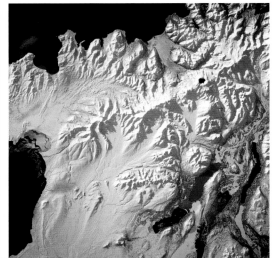

26 TOP RIGH THE KATMAI NATIONAL PARK LANDSCAPE HAS BEEN SHAPED BY GLACIERS WHICH HAVE CARVED OUT DEEP VALLEYS AND FORMED GREAT LAKES.

26-27 THE PERIOD IN WHICH THE TERRAIN IS ALMOST COMPLETELY FREE OF SNOW IS SHORT. BY OCTOBER SNOW ALREADY STARTS TO ACCUMULATE ON THE TUNDRA AND IN THE FORESTS.

27 GRIZZLY BEARS ARE ONE OF THE PARK'S PROTECTED SPECIES.

Katmai National Park and Preserve
Alaska

The northernmost part of the Pacific, where the Asian and American continents almost touch, is one of the Earth's richest and most vital areas, a true common ground between the Palearctic and Nearctic. Particularly interesting is the long Alaskan peninsula, extending out into the seas, continuing into the Aleutian Islands archipelago. Here, during World War II (in May 1943), Americans troops fought a fierce battle against Japanese invaders.

Today the area is protected by a large national park (420,000 acres/170,000 hectares) dedicated to the conservation of important animal species: moose, caribou, wolves, and especially grizzly bears. This species has special skills that enable it to make the most of the desolate but productive coastal marine environment in the search for food. In fact, the bears on the coast of Katmai Park feed where the waves hit the shores, dedicating themselves with stubborn determination to the gathering of 'seafood' that the waves wash up onto the beaches.

The density of the bear population is exceptional, so much so that in neighboring areas the species is hunted, but the parkwide protection system, which has been in place for many years, makes the bears confident; they are visible and easily observed by a growing number of naturalists and visitors.

The region and the park's vegetation is composed of species typical of the tundra: maiden's-tears and other plants with profuse summer flowering are common; in the most humid lowlands; where there is some fertile soil and where the rocks block the gusts of wind, creeping arctic willow bushes grow; and in the marshes cotton grass abounds, recognizable by its typical white plumes. In addition, the park is home to many of lichens, ferns and mosses typical of permafrost (permanently frozen) terrain. Fauna includes 40 mammal species and almost 200 bird species.

The park, with its magnificent glacial landscapes, its stretches of tundra and marine shores populated by thousands of birds that make their nests in crowded colonies, is caught in the grip of the cold for most of the year. However, it bursts into life from June to July, the period of the brief but intense arctic summer. During this time, the tundra's small plants flower, the caribou give birth to their young, the bears and their cubs wander in search of food and birds tend to their broods.

The spectacular "Valley of Ten Thousand Smokes" (into which volcanic steam and ash vent) offers striking and primordial scenery in which signs of man are imperceptible and natural phenomena follow their own rhythms, completely undisturbed, as they did 10,000 years ago.

Katmai

28 TOP LARGELY OF VOLCANIC ORIGIN, THE KATMAI TERRITORY STILL CONTAINS A BIG CALDERA, A COLLAPSED AREA OVER A MAGMA CHAMBER, WHICH HAS STEEP ROCKY SIDES.

28 BOTTOM WOLVES REMAIN IN THE ARCTIC REGION EVEN DURING WINTER. HOWEVER, THEY MOVE SOUTH, FOLLOWING THE MIGRATING CARIBOU HERDS.

28-29 THE BALD EAGLE, SYMBOL OF THE UNITES STATES OF AMERICA, NESTS. THESE "HOMES" CAN EXTEND TO 6.5 FT (2 M) IN WIDTH.

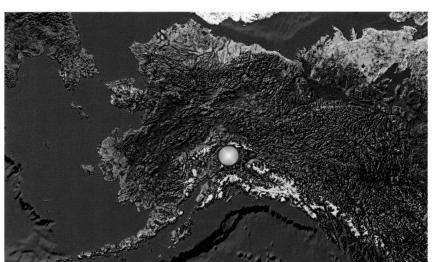

Denali National Park and Preserve
Alaska

Denali National Park in Alaska is the home park of the grizzly bear, the largest North American mammal, which is well known because it congregates in large numbers on the riverbanks during the period when salmon swim upstream to deposit their eggs near the springs. The fascinating spectacle of dozens of grizzlies crowding the riverbanks attracts photographers and admirers from all over the world; they also have a chance of photographing the bald eagle, another able hunter of salmon, and the symbol of the United States of America.

The wildlife of this park of mountain terrain and tundra also includes the wolf, moose, and elk, which during mating season in the fall, engage in violent antler duels and roaring contests to win the right to mate with the females. The national park and preserve extends over 6 million acres (2.5 million hectares) in a harsh and difficult land of endless winter and brief summers, barely warmed by the sun that lies low on the horizon. It is intended to protect the almost uncontaminated sub-arctic area that spreads over inner Alaska, in the shadow of mighty Mt. McKinley (20,000 ft/6096 m), the tallest mountain in North America, called "Denali," or "Tall One" by the Athabaskans, the Native Americans of the region. It is a mountain of bold shapes, formed by various blocks of rock, each different in origin and formation. This explains the wonderful colors that can be admired from the Polychrome Pass.

The park is located in the Alaskan Range, an extensive natural barrier more than 620 miles (1000 km) long, still in a state of orogenic upheaval, covered by glaciers, snow, tundra and taiga. A grouping of extensive faults, known as the Denali Fault, surrounds the Alaskan Range and is the cause of the thousands of earthquakes that are registered in the area every year.

Temperatures in the park region are generally low, even in summer, and in winter sink to -58° F (-50° C), with winds that can exceed 150 miles (240 km) per hour. Vegetation is composed of plants typical of the tundra and plants that force themselves from the subsoil up through the surface pebbles, and selenes and other plants that bloom intensely in the short summer. In the humid wetlands, where there is some fertile soil and where the rocks block the quick gusts of wind, creeping bushes of Arctic willow grow; and then, in the morass, cotton grass grows with its typical white plumes.

The park census records more than 60 species of flowering plants, along with many types of lichens, ferns, and mosses typical of permafrost areas.

Wildlife includes 40 mammal species, almost 200 bird species, 10 fish species, and one species of amphibian indigenous to the Denali zone.

The park was established as Mt. McKinley National Park in 1917; it became an International Biosphere Reserve in 1976; and in 1980, with enlargement, changed its name and became Denali National Park.

30 TOP RIGHT A FEMALE MOOSE WITH ITS YOUNG WALKS ON A SNOW-COVERED AREA.

30-31 ONE OF THE MOST SPECTACULAR PEAKS IN DENALI NATIONAL PARK, IS THE "MOOSE TOOTH," WHICH IS A COVETED TARGET OF CLIMBERS.

31 SNOW ACCUMULATES ON THE MOUNTAIN PEAKS AND THE PLUNGES DOWN IN THE FORM OF SLIDES AND AVALANCHES.

Denali

32-33 AND 33 TOP THOUGH CONIFEROUS TREES LIKE PINES AND FIRS CONSERVE THEIR DENSE AND ODOROUS NEEDLE-LIKE LEAVES THROUGHOUT THE WINTER, SHRUBS SHED THEIR LEAVES AFTER HAVING TAKEN ON VIVID COLORS.

33 BOTTOM WITH THE ARRIVAL OF THE MATING SEASON THE LAYER OF SKIN WHICH COVERS AND NOURISHES THE MALE MOOSE ANTLERS IS SHED AND IS REPLACED BY DEADLY ANTLERS WHICH THEY USE IN THEIR FIGHTS.

34-35 MOUNT MCKINLEY IS THE HIGHEST PEAK IN NORTH AMERICA. IT DOMINATES DENALI NATIONAL PARK WITH ITS SNOWY CRESTS AND ITS BIG GLACIERS.

36-37 THE AURORA BOREALIS, A PHENOMENON WHICH IS PARTICULARLY EVIDENT IN THE LONG ARCTIC NIGHTS, HAS IMPRESSED GENERATIONS OF TRAVELERS AND HAS GIVEN BIRTH TO MYTHS AND TRADITIONS STILL ALIVE IN THE CULTURE OF THE NATIVES.

37 TOP HUMANKIND HAS SPENT MANY CENTURIES TRYING TO DECIPHER THE ORIGIN OF THE AURORA BOREALIS WHICH CHARACTERIZES THE NIGHT SKIES OF ALL ARCTIC REGIONS.

37 BOTTOM IN THE MIDDLE OF THE NIGHT, THE COLORS OF THE AURORA BOREALIS SEEMS TO REPRODUCE IN THE SKY THE COLORS OF THE TUNDRA AT THE APPROACH OF WINTER.

Wrangell-St. Elias National Park and Preserve

Alaska

The three large mountain ranges – the Wrangell, Chugach and St. Elias – converge in this park, which includes more than 100 glaciers; among these is the vast Hubbard Glacier that forms deep in the Yukon and reaches the sea in the Bay of Disenchantment – after traveling more than 100 miles (160 km) and joining with the Valerie Glacier to the west.

The movements and cycles of expansion and contraction of the ice have strongly influenced the land of the park in the last millennia; in fact, in 1986 the Hubbard Glacier completely closed off Russell fjord, creating the short-lived "Lake Russell." During the summer the lake rose more than 82 ft (25 m) and the water lost its salt content: what was initially a basin of ocean water became a freshwater lake until October of the same year, when a dike formed by the glacier broke. In less than a day, more than 176 billion cu. ft (5 billion cu. m) of water poured back into the ocean with which the fjord was again connected.

The flora and fauna of the park are of the arctic and sub-arctic type, with a limited number of species that are, however, of great interest not only for scientists but also for visitors who venture into this area. There is a large population of Dall sheep, a distant relative of the moufflon whose origins date back to a herd that lived in Asia and migrated to America in ancient times over the Bering Strait, which was then a bridge of ice. Along with the more common and smaller black bear, this is the region frequented by the grizzly bear, the American towering brown bear of well-known predatory skills. Besides salmon, which the bear catches in the water when they swim upstream to deposit their eggs, the grizzly also hunts caribou, elk and moose. Other predatory mammals include the lynx and the wolf, working in packs to catch deer and caribou, their principal prey.

In the coastal area, killer whales concentrate, attracted by the large number of salmon, whales, sea lions and sea otters.

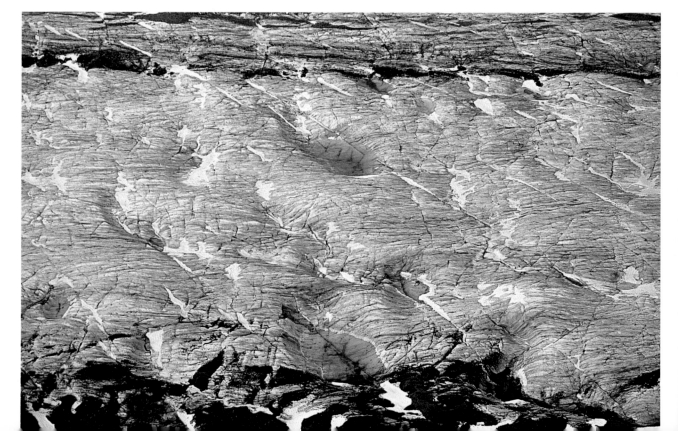

38 SMALL LAKES ARE FORMED EVERY YEAR WITH THE INCREASE IN TEMPERATURE AND THE MELTING OF THE SNOW ON THE GLACIERS.

38-39 THE GLACIERS IN THE ARCTIC REGIONS OF NORTH AMERICA ARE IN A PHASE OF REGRESSION LIKE THOSE OF THE ALPS AND THE HIMALAYAS.

39 TOP RIGHT THE EXPANSE OF THE GLACIER NEAR CHISANA.

40-41 THE SNOWY PEAKS OF THE PARK IN THE EVENING LIGHT.

Wrangell-St. Elias

42-43 THE HUBBARD GLACIER IS ONE OF THE MOST IMPORTANT IN ALASKA. GIGANTIC ICEBERGS
CONTINUALLY BREAK OFF FROM ITS FACADE, WHICH IS OVER 150 FT (45 M) IN HEIGHT.

43 TOP ORCA WHALES ARE FOUND IN COASTAL WATERS WHERE LARGE CONCENTRATIONS OF SALMON,
AN IMPORTANT FOOD RESOURCE FOR THESE PREDATORS, ARE FOUND.

43 BOTTOM THE GLACIER IS GRADUALLY STARTING TO MELT DOWN AND LIBERATE THE TUNDRA
AND THE PLAINS TO THE WATERBED OF ST. ELIAS MOUNTAINS.

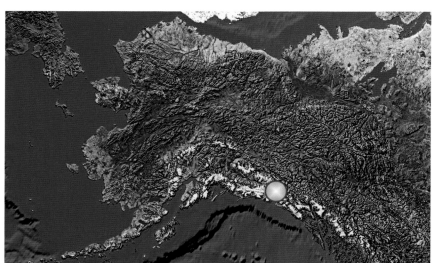

Glacier Bay National Park
Alaska

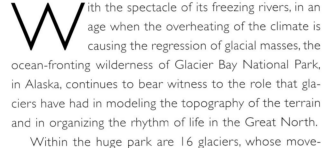

With the spectacle of its freezing rivers, in an age when the overheating of the climate is causing the regression of glacial masses, the ocean-fronting wilderness of Glacier Bay National Park, in Alaska, continues to bear witness to the role that glaciers have had in modeling the topography of the terrain and in organizing the rhythm of life in the Great North.

Within the huge park are 16 glaciers, whose movements and characteristics are studied in a magnificent setting which ranges from mountain ranges to fjords, to icebergs and floes, and from rocky coasts to the open sea. The region's glaciers have not been immune to global warning, and shrinkage is being recorded; the situation of two centuries ago, when the sea was often completely covered in ice, is long gone. When Britain's Captain George Vancouver mapped this area in 1794, present-day Glacier Bay was a simple nook of about five miles in front of a giant glacier that extended for more than 125 miles (200 km) down from the Mount St. Elias mountain range. As early as 1879, John Muir discovered that the ice had retreated almost 37 miles (60 km), uncovering the present-day bay that, freed from the masses of ice, continues to record a rise in the water level.

The Glacier Bay region reflects a dynamic landscape, in constant change, that has strongly influenced the habitats that sustain animal and plant life of all types, from the sub-arctic to the mountainous, and from the coastal to the forest. Marine life is especially plentiful because ocean currents and fresh water, rich in nutrients coming from the coast, feed the food chain at whose top are predators such as the killer whale and sea lion, while most whales species feed on plankton and small-sized marine organisms. Particularly conspicuous is the presence of the humpback whale, the large whale with a hump, which can reach 60 ft (18 m) in length.

The park was established in 1980, although the bay was already protected as a National Monument in 1925; it was named a Wilderness Area in 1980, a Biosphere Reserve in 1986; and a World Heritage Site in 1992.

46 TOP A GROUP OF SEA LIONS POSITIONED ON ROCKS GET READY TO CATCH FISH.

46 BOTTOM EVERY SUMMER HUMPBACK WHALES RETURN BACK TO THE BAY AFTER HAVING COMPLETED A LONG MIGRATION FROM THE SOUTHERN SEAS IN SEARCH FOR FOOD. THESE WATERS ARE PARTICULARLY RICH IN PLANKTON AND OF OTHER SMALL MARINE ORGANISMS.

47 A LONG STRIP OF ICE FLANKS THE SIDES OF THE PARK'S SNOWY TERRAIN AND EXTENDS TO THE SHORELINE.

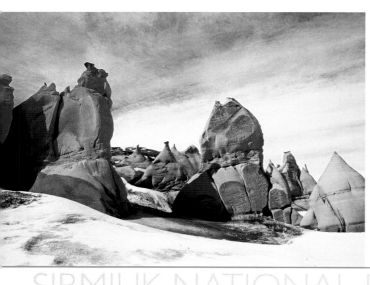

48 TOP LEFT ROCKS SCULPTED BY WIND ARE A COMMON CHARACTERISTIC OF THE COASTS WHICH ARE MORE EXPOSED TO THE CURRENTS.

48-49 PART OF THE PARK'S MOUNTAIN CHAIN IS A CONTINUATION OF THE ARCTIC MOUNTAIN RANGE WHICH EXTENDS FROM BAFFIN ISLAND TO ELLESMERE ISLAND.

49 THE COMPACTION AND CRYSTALLIZATION OF THE SNOW CREATES DIFFERENTLY SHAPED FORMS SUCH AS GLACIERS WHICH ARE SIMILAR TO STALACTITES AND ARE FORMED BY THE DRIPPING WATER.

Sirmilik National Park
Nunavut

Dedicated to the nature of the Great North, Sirmilik National Park for most of the year is transformed into a desolate expanse of snow and ice swept by blizzard winds, with temperatures that regularly dip to under 40° below zero. In fact, "Sirmilik" is an Inuktitut word that means, "the place of the glaciers." This is the world of the Aurora Borealis, the luminous phenomenon that for a few moments lights up the sky with yellow, purple, blue and green hues.

The park, which was established in 2001, protects about 8600 sq miles (22,275 sq. km) and includes four different areas: Bylot Island, Borden Peninsula, Baillarge Bay and Oliver Sound. High mountains and glaciers account for most of the park, although tundra extends over a substantial area. Some peaks are part of the Arctic Mountains, which extend from Baffin Island to Ellesmere Island.

Most of the birds typical of the Arctic region spend the summer in the park area; 74 species have been cataloged or identified, of which 45 are nesting birds. Bylot Island is considered a sanctuary for migratory birds, some of which build nests at the top of ocean cliffs, between Cape Hay and Cape Graham. Oliver Sound and Borden Peninsula offer breathtaking views, among the most beautiful in the entire the region.

Among the park's most interesting features are the hoodoos, dramatic geological formations that are high towers of sedimentary rock worn away over millennia by ice, water and wind. Also of interest are the many polynyas, areas of open sea among the glaciers. They are caused by various environmental factors such as the rising of water from the ocean floor, currents and winds. Polynyas do not freeze even in winter; thus, they are a haven for many animals: belugas, seals and polar bears.

Lancaster Sound is one of the most productive and vital marine areas in the entire Arctic: besides birds there are also polar bears and many species of seals and whales. Every year the narwhals, mysterious dolphins with a long tusk that inspired the legend of the unicorn, gather in these waters and the males challenge each other with their weapons as if they were swords. The Sound, which is the most eastern part of the so-called Northwest Passage, is an important route for transport and commerce.

The park represents an area where it is possible to enjoy the beauty of many geomorphologic surfaces of glacial origin: moraines, icebergs, permafrost, glacial cirques, pingos (small hills), sandy deposits and rock cones.

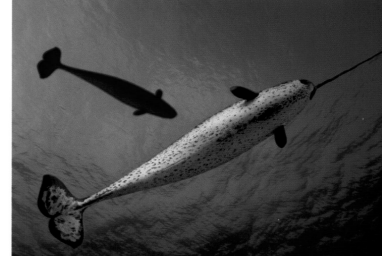

50-51 AND 51 NARWHALS (ALSO
KNOWN AS MOON WHALES) ARE FOUND
EXCLUSIVELY IN THE COLD ARCTIC
OCEANS. THEY ARE CHARACTERIZED
BY A SINGLE TUSK WHICH IS
EXTRAORDINARY LONG AND WHICH
IS USED IN FIGHTS DURING THEIR
MATING SEASON.

52-53 A SOLITARY BEAR STROLLS IN THE
PARK'S HUGE EXPANSE. THE
GEOMORPHIC PROTRUSIONS OF GLACIAL
ORIGIN ARE PARTICULARLY EVIDENT
IN ALL THE TERRITORY: MORAINES,
ICEBERGS, PERMAFROST, GLACIER
VALLEYS, PINGOS, SANDY AND
CONOIDAL DEPOSITS.

Mount Robson Provincial Park

British Columbia

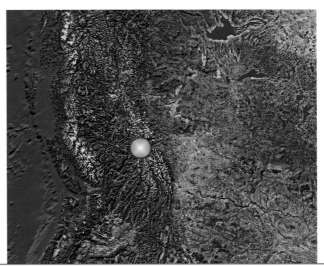

Mount Robson Park is one of the oldest protected areas in British Columbia and in Canada as a whole, and encompasses 553,516 acres (224,866 hectares) of almost virgin land. At the heart of the protected territory is the immense mass of Mount Robson, which reaches a height of 12,792 ft (3954 m) and is the highest mountaintop of the Rocky Mountains in British Columbia. The peaks and its approaches are characterized by imposing snowfields and glaciers. Of the latter, the Berg Glacier is considered one of the most 'living' in all of North America. Glaciologists who have been tracking it happily report that contrary to the usual finding in this age of global warning, the Berg Glacier does not appear to be diminishing. In fact, it appears to be getting larger year by year, in welcome contrast to other glaciers in the rest of the world. The springs of the Frazer River, one of the most important rivers in British Columbia, rise in the park and flow raucously through thick forests of shrubs and deciduous trees that gradually give way to dense woods of beeches and pine. The wildlife of the protected area includes almost all of North America's indigenous large mammal species: the grizzly, the black bear – which can be easily observed fishing for salmon in the Fraser River rapids at Echo Harbor – the wolf, the wolverine, the coyote and the fisher, as well as stoats, otters and other water-loving species that hunt small animals on the river banks. Among the herbivores are the elk, Rocky Mountain sheep, or Bighorns, and the mountain goat with its immaculate mantle. There are also moose present; among hoofed animals they are the most aquatic, searching for edible grasses in the shallows of even the deepest lakes.

Mount Robson Park's avifauna includes 190 species of birds; among them are the sea eagle, the golden eagle, the peregrine falcon, the goshawk, the American eagle-owl, and wild turkey, geese, pheasant and woodpeckers and other birds that live in mountainous and woodland areas. In 1990, UNESCO designated the park as part of the Canadian Rocky Mountains World Heritage Site.

54 TOP BERG GLACIER AND BERG LAKE IN MOUNT ROBSON PROVINCIAL PARK, BRITISH COLUMBIA.

54-55 AND 55 BOTTOM MOUNT ROBSON, 12,792 FT (3954 M) HIGH, IS THE HIGHEST POINT OF THE CANADIAN ROCKIES.

55 CENTER MOUNT ROBSON PARK IS CONSIDERED AS A WILDERNESS BECAUSE IT IS COMPLETELY DEVOID OF ANY HUMAN PRESENCE.

56-57 MOUNT ROBSON, SEEN FROM MARMOT CAMP ON THE TRAIL TO BERG LAKE.

58 TOP A BLACK BEAR CATCHES SALMON IN THE RAPIDS OF A TORRENT IN ECHO HARBOR.

58-59 THE FRAZER RIVER FLOWS TURBULENTLY AMID DENSE FIR AND PINE FORESTS.

59 TOP OF THE DEER SPECIES, THE MOOSE IS THE MEMBER MOST DRAWN TO WATER, EVEN VENTURING IN DEEP WATERS TO GRAZE WATER PLANTS.

59 BOTTOM THE FISHER IS AN AQUATIC MARTEN AND HUNTS FOR SMALL ANIMALS ON THE SHORES OF STREAMS.

60 TOP LEFT THE COYOTE LEADS A MAINLY SOLITARY LIFE.

60 TOP RIGHT THE EMERALD LAKE REFLECTING THE IMAGES OF THE SNOWY PEAKS IN THE HEART OF THE PARK.

60-61 DENSE FORESTS OF FIR AND PINE TREES COVER YOHO PARK'S LOWER TERRAIN WHICH, BY SEPTEMBER, ALREADY GAINS A WINTRY APPEARANCE.

Yoho National Park
British Columbia

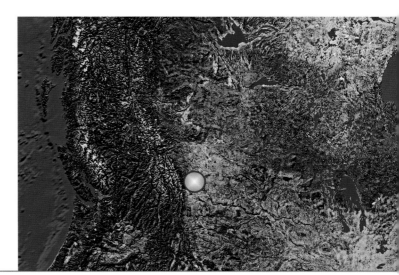

Situated on the border between the provinces of Alberta and British Columbia, Yoho National Park (324,450 acres/131,000 hectares) is famous not only for its spectacular landscapes of glacial origin, but also for the many treasures of the past that it holds in its Burgess shale and other rock strata. Here, in fact, were found the fossil remains of 120 species of marine animals of the Cambrian period, dating back approximately 515 million years. This trove remains a true cornucopia for paleontologists, geologists, and earth scientists.

Snowy peaks, cirques, small lakes and dense forests of larches, pines and beeches at the lower altitudes characterize most of the landscape of the park which, as a result of erosion, displays some interesting geological phenomena. These include natural bridges and arches of rock, such as the spectacular bridge over Kicking Horse River and the hoodoos, the odd formations dotting areas of terrain where blocks of stone rest on very high columns of sediment deposited by glaciers.

Of great beauty are the numerous striking waterfalls which feed Yoho National Park's many rivers; these, in turn, are a valuable resource; many contain salmon.

The mighty Columbia River flows through the protected territory, making its way through rocks covered with lichens of a thousands different colors. Lakes abound, and the water of the charming Emerald Lake is so calm that it reflects the smallest details of the snow-capped peaks. Lake O'Hara Valley is another attraction: it is the park's most picturesque because of its typical glacial origins and is backdrops of serried mountain peaks covered in dense forests of larches.

The wildlife of the protected area includes many species of carnivorous animals, among them grizzly bears and black bears, puma, the wolverine — one of the strongest predators of the Rocky Mountains — and skunks and weasels. The park is also home to an important population of Canadian lynx; they inhabit the woody areas where they hunt rabbit and deer.

61 CENTER AT DAWN ROCKS ASSUME A DELICATE VIOLET COLOR FROM THE GRADUALLY CLEARING SKY.

61 BOTTOM WINTER IS A PROPITIOUS SEASON FOR THE LYNCH: ITS PREYS' MOVEMENTS ARE ENCUMBERED BY SNOW MAKING THEM MORE VULNERABLE FOR THIS PREDATOR.

Yoho

62 O'HARA LAKE IS FOUND IN THE WESTERN SIDE OF THE NATIONAL PARK. MOUNT HUBER IS SEEN IN THE BACKGROUND.

63 TOP A FEMALE LYNX PROTECTS ITS CUB. THE LYNX LIVES IN WOODS WHERE IT HUNTS FOR HARES AND DEAR.

63 BOTTOM A WATERFALL POURS OUT WATER ON ONE OF THE NUMEROUS TORRENTS WHICH FLOW IN YOHO NATIONAL PARK. SALMONID INHABIT SEVERAL OF THESE TORRENTS.

64-65 THE WAPTA MOUNTAIN' REFLECTION IN THE CALM WATERS OF EMERALD LAKE.

Glacier National Park
British Columbia/Montana

Rainfall is the element that regulates the rhythm of life and alters the landscape of this vast protected area (1 million acres/410,000 hectares) that is found in the Columbia Mountain Region, between the first coastal relief to the west and the Canadian Rocky Mountains to the east. Masses of humid air coming from the Pacific, pushed by often violent and persistent winds, are intercepted by the walls of the Columbia Mountain Range and cause strong rains in the summer and heavy snowfall in winter.

Water favors the development of thick vegetation, of a temperate rainforest, which – if it were not for the cold temperatures even in summer and the harsh ones during the winter – would have much in common with tropical forests. Here, too, as in the tropics, the tree level dominates the ecosystem with gigantic pines and other conifers that tower over a carpet of ferns and mosses. Ancient trees fall to the ground and are slowly broken down by mushrooms, insects, and invertebrate life forms: one can almost hear the work of millions of insects and other forms of life that bit by bit consume the organic material and return it the soil.

A high level of rainfall, the accumulation of snow and relatively moderate temperatures are the dominant characteristics not only of the area related to the forest, but also of the remaining part of the territory which has 50 percent of its surface above the tree line. Here glaciers cover more than 10 percent of the surface. True vegetation is nearly absent; the environment is dominated by lichens, mosses and a small number of specially adapted plants that grow, compact and creeping, attached to rocks to withstand the fury of the wind and to maximize the heat furnished by a sun that is often feeble and obscured by a persistent cloak of clouds and/or fog.

Animal life is varied: grizzlies and black bears, woodchucks, pika, squirrels, and mountain caribou are all present. Beavers abound in the few humid areas, which are found only along the narrow valleys of the Selkirk Mountains. Here the beavers modify the river ecosystems with their incessant activity, building dams that slow the strong torrential currents and create charming ponds surrounded by tall conifers.

66 APPARENTLY DEVOID OF LIFE, THE PEAKS OF THE CANADIAN ROCKIES ARE IN FACT INHABITED BY BIGHORNS, LYNXES, PRAIRIE DOGS AND MANY OTHER SPECIES.

66-67 AND 67 TOP LEFT THE MOUNTAIN RANGE ON THE CANADIAN-AMERICAN BORDER IS A DISTINGUISHING FEATURE OF THE PARK'S LANDSCAPE. THE PEAKS ARE COVERED BY SNOW FOR THE MAJOR PART OF THE YEAR BECAUSE OF THEIR GREAT HEIGHTS AND LOW TEMPERATURE.

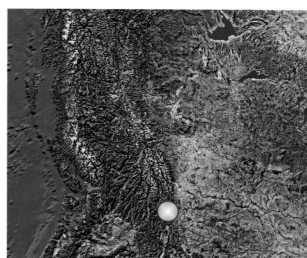

Glacier

68 A MULE DEER HIDES IN THE WOODS. THIS ANIMAL IS WIDESPREAD IN THE WESTERN PARTS OF NORTH AMERICA AND IS RECOGNIZABLE BY ITS LARGE EARS WHICH LOOK LIKE THOSE OF A MULE, HENCE ITS NAME.

68-69 RED AND YELLOW, THE COLORS OF FALL, EXCELLENTLY CHARACTERIZE THE PARK'S WOODLAND SCENERY AT THE END OF THE SEASON. IN THE BACKGROUND, THE PEAKS WITH THEIR PERENNIAL SNOW.

69 TOP LEFT A STREAM FORMS A SMALL WATERFALL ON MOUNT CANNON. ALL THE PROTECTED AREA IS RICH IN STREAMS AND LAKES WHOSE WATER DERIVES COPIOUS RAIN SHOWERS WHICH OCCUR IN THIS TERRITORY IN AUTUMN.

69 TOP CENTER GROUND SQUIRRELS LIVE IN BURROWS DUG IN THE TERRAIN WHERE THEY STORE FOOD IN ORDER TO SURVIVE THE WINTER.

69 TOP RIGHT A DENSE PINE FOREST FLANKS THE FLATHEAD RIVER IN THE STATE OF MONTANA.

Glacier

70 DEEPLY ALTERED BY WATER, WIND AND OTHER WEATHERING FACTORS,
THE GLACIER NATIONAL PARK'S TERRITORY REMINDS ONE OF THE ICE AGE'S
PRIMITIVE SCENES.

71 TOP THE GRINNEL LAKE IS SITUATED IN A PROTECTED VALLEY AND
IS CHARACTERIZED BY ITS WATER'S CRYSTALLINE COLOR.

71 BOTTOM THE MOUNTAIN GOAT LIVES EXCLUSIVELY IN VERY HIGH PEAKS.
ITS THICK FUR WHICH PROTECTS IT FROM THE COLD.

72-73 A SUMMER STORM IS ABOUT TO BREAK OVER SHERBURNE LAKE.

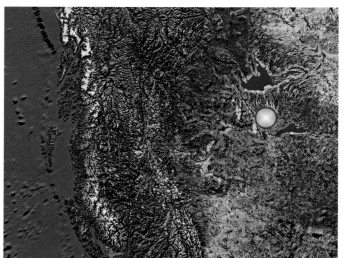

74 TOP LEFT STREAMS MAKE THEIR WAY WITH TWISTING PATHS IN THE TUNDRA AND TAIGA TERRITORY.

74-75 WOOD BUFFALO NATIONAL PARK IS VAST, UNINHABITED AND DEVOID OF MEANS OF ACCESS.

75 LAKE CLAIRE IS ONE OF THE LARGEST LAKES OF THE PROTECTED TERRITORY, WHICH HAS ENSURED THE SURVIVAL OF MANY THREATENED ANIMAL SPECIES OF THE GREAT AMERICAN NORTH.

Wood Buffalo National Park
Alberta/Northwestern Territories

In the 19th century, the North American plains were home to some 60 million bison. These enormous animals moved in great herds, migrating in search of better pastures in a vast area that included prairie lands and, in the higher latitudes, part of the Great Northern Forest. Bison were the base of a food pyramid that supplied nutrition not only for grizzly bears, wolves and other predators, but also for numerous native peoples who hunted the bison itself, but with methods that allowed the herds to maintain themselves in good numbers.

With the advent of European colonization this natural balance was destined to be short lived. The tragic story of the American bison is well known: in the 19th century the new European settlers wiped the herds with systematic ferocity, killing the animals not only for their flesh, but purposefully to eliminate the food source of many Indian populations. At the end of the 1800s only a few hundred of bison remained, and it was only then that hunting was belatedly but thankfully forbidden. From that moment a slow process of recovery began, one that – even if it could not restore the "great herd" – could restore the presence of the bison in many protected areas.

Today the biggest herd lives freely in the largest protected area of Canada, the Wood Buffalo National Park, which spreads out from Lake Athabasca. Present here is the very population of what is defined as the wood bison *(Bison bison athabascae)*, whose hooves are more developed, whose horns are longer, and whose coat is darker than the prairie bison. They are the animals most closely associated with the marshy and partially woody environments that constitute the heart of the protected territory where the grasslands and the northern forest meet.

The Wood Buffalo National Park, which was established in 1922, is Canada's largest protected area. It is located between Alberta and the Northwest Territories, to the south of the Great Slave, and extends over 17,300 sq. miles (44,807 sq. km). The park's lands are so vast and uninhabited that in many areas the borders were drawn using airplanes. It has three typical ecosystems: forests of white spruce, poplar, and pine typical of sub-

Arctic regions; plateaus sprinkled with rivers, streams and ponds; and the delta formed by the Peace and Athabasca Rivers, which flow into Lake Athabasca. It is one of the largest freshwater deltas in the world and because of this is one of the most important and beautiful inland humid zones. The presence of ancient, predominately calcareous and gypsum rock from the Devonian period underneath glacial deposits of varying thickness gives rise to extraordinary systems of subterranean grottos and rivers caused by karsism (the water-caused erosion of certain limestone strata) and by salt springs, salt fields and salty mudflats – the only ones known in Canada. In particularly dry years, blocks of salt as tall as 6.5 ft (2 m) form around the springs.

The park and its large inland humid zone have also contributed to the safeguarding of another rare and endangered species: the American whooping crane. In 1940 only a dozen or so of these birds remained; today there are more than 150. The park seems to be the only area in the world where this species nests, along with the rare peregrine falcon and other migratory birds.

Wood Buffalo

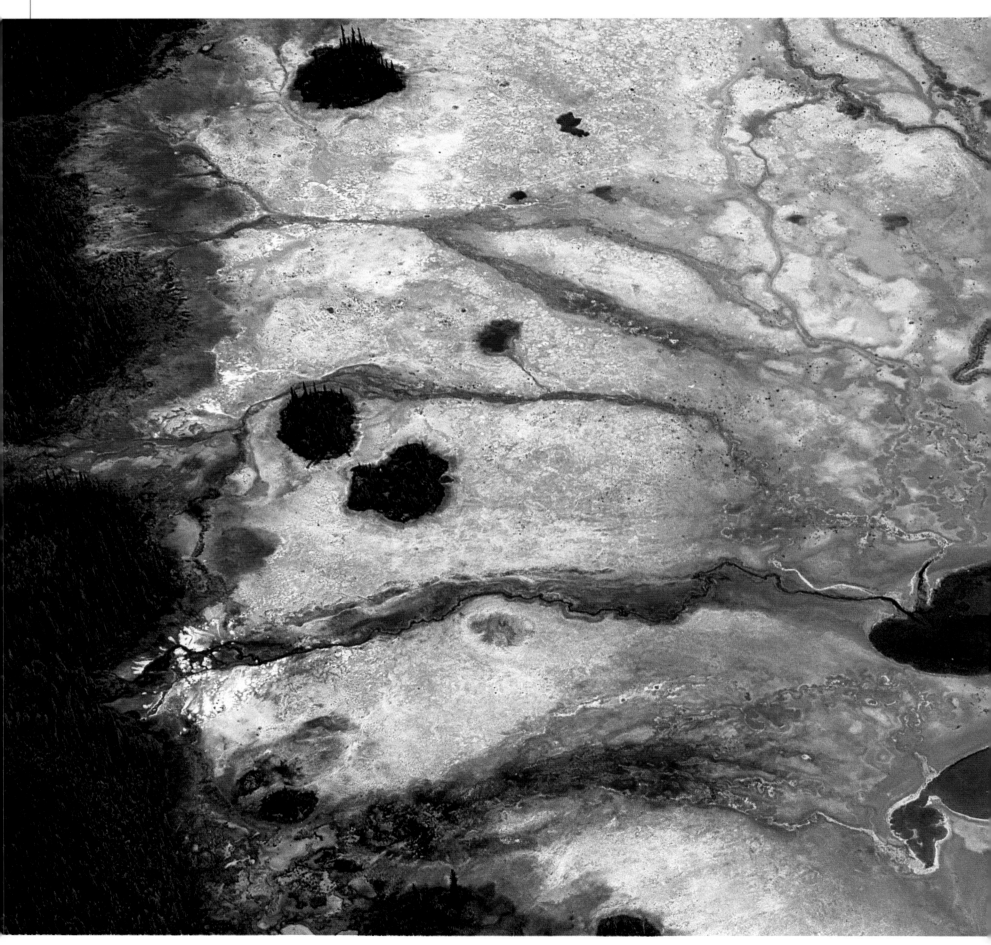

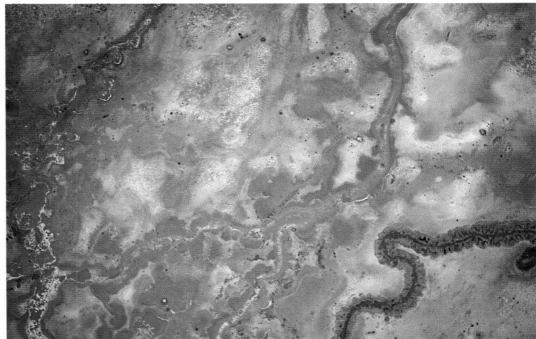

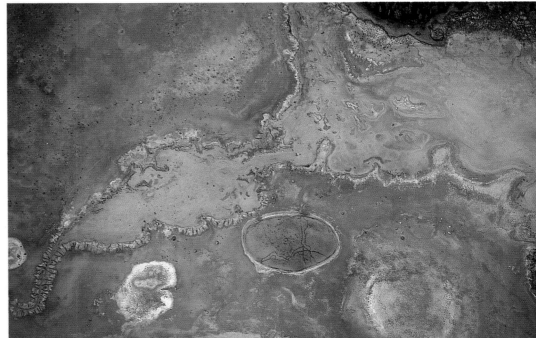

76-77 AND 77 CRYSTALS FROM THE SALTY BASINS SEDIMENT THEMSELVES AND FORM DAINTY CRUSTS WHICH ASSUME THE COLORS OF THE RAINBOW WHEN LIGHT HITS THEM. SOME AREAS, WHERE THE SALINE CONCENTRATIONS ARE LESS HIGH, BECOME IMPORTANT STOPS FOR 'SWAMP' BIRDS AND SHOREBIRDS DURING THEIR LONG MIGRATORY JOURNEYS.

Wood Buffalo

78 MANY BASINS ARE STILL SITUATED IN AREAS SO REMOTE THAT THEIR EXPLORATION CAN BE CONSIDERED AS STILL IN ITS BEGINNINGS.

79 TOP AND CENTER WOOD BUFFALO NATIONAL PARK HOSTS A CONSISTENT NUMBER OF WOOD BISON, ANIMALS WHICH ARE WELL ADAPTED IN LIVING IN THE CLOSED ENVIRONMENTS OF THE TAIGA EVEN IN THE HEIGHT OF THE WINTER SEASON.

79 BOTTOM ELKS START TO MATE AT THE END OF SUMMER. MALE ELKS BELLOW TO SIGNAL THEIR PRESENCE TO THE FEMALES AND CHALLENGE EACH OTHER IN EXHAUSTING BATTLES.

Banff and Jasper National Parks
Alberta

In a barren, rocky landscape, where huge rocks alternate with stretches of ice and spring snow that lasts all summer long, under a sky at times so blue it seems black, the agile and characteristic shape of mountain goats can be seen, enveloped in their white coats. These ungulates are perfectly adapted to life among the rocks and ice; their cloven hooves are equipped with adhesive pads to make their footing more secure. These are the most typical animals of the vast protected area formed by two neighboring national parks, Banff National Park and Jasper National Park, located in Western Canada on the ridge of the Canadian Rocky Mountains, and extending over Alberta and British Columbia. Together they cover an area of approximately 6744 sq. miles (17,466 sq. km), adding up to one of the world's largest wilderness areas, in whose uncontaminated environment man's presence is nonexistent. Banff National Park extends over about 2564 sq. miles (6641 sq. km). It was Canada's first national park and was established in 1885 to safeguard the hot springs typical of many areas of the northern Rocky Mountains. Jasper National Park, covering about 4200 sq. miles (10,878 sq. km),

Canada's most northerly protected area, was established in 1930 and was later designated a World Heritage Site by UNESCO. A large fault, 10 miles (16 km) wide and more than 925 miles (1490 km) long, separates the two national parks from British Columbia's the oldest mountain range, which lies to the west. The terrain is uniquely marked by a large system of glaciers, the Columbia Icefield, an extraordinary array of ice masses that extend over 202 sq. miles (325 sq. km), with an average thickness of 1000 ft (304 m). This ice field constitutes the apex North America's hydrographic system in that the waters of its catchment basins and from the partial melting of the glaciers flow from a single point to three different oceans. The ice masses that feed the Columbia and Frazer rivers flow into to the Pacific Ocean; the Saskatchewan River flows into Hudson Bay, and the Slave, Mackenzie and Athabasca rivers debouch into the Arctic Ocean. The Athabasca River and its tributaries drain four-fifths of the protected area. Set among the mountains are a number of lakes, among which the most famous is Lake Louise, with the Victoria Glacier in the background. The presence of Mount Columbia (12,400 feet/3780 m) is also worth noting. The two parks host three different eco-regions (mountainous, alpine and sub-alpine), and many forms of animal and plant life typical of the Arctic and high mountain zones. The fauna includes the bear, elk, caribou, mountain goat, cougar, wolf, coyote, woodchuck and pika. In total, the parks host some 69 mammals, 40 species of fish, 16 amphibians and reptiles, and about 2000 species of insects and spiders. Bird species total 277, including ptarmigan, spruce grouse, various hawks, ravens, crows, mountain chickadees and many other birds of interest. Flora includes over 1300 species of plants. Jasper Park is unique in that it has only sandy dune ecosystem (the Jasper Lake Dunes) in the four Canadian mountain parks as well as having the northernmost boundary, where the Douglas fir is found, and the most extensive subterranean hydrographic system in Canada – the Maligne Valley Karst system. The mountain caribou, symbol of the Columbia Mountains and a relative of the reindeer and the tundra caribou, is present but in such small numbers that it is considered at risk of becoming of extinct.

80 THE TWO PARKS HOST FLORA AND
FAUNA COMMUNITIES WHICH BELONG
TO THE ALPINE, SUB-ALPINE AND
MOUNTAINOUS ECO-REGIONS.

80-81 AND 81 TOP RIGHT THIS AREA
IS THE APEX OF THE NORTH AMERICAN
HYDROGRAPHIC SYSTEM SINCE THE
WATERS OF ITS RAINY BASINS FLOW
TOWARDS 3 DIFFERENT OCEANS.

82-83 SET BETWEEN THE MOUNTAINS
ARE SEVERAL LAKES OF GLACIAL ORIGIN;
THEY DISAPPEAR DURING THE WINTER
UNDER A LAYER OF ICE.

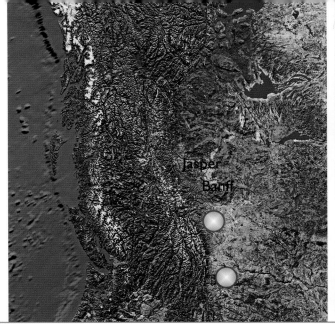

84 A WATERFALL MAKES ITS WAY BETWEEN ROCKS AND SNOW, ITS WATERS DERIVING FROM THE FUSION OF GLACIERS AND SNOWFIELDS. IN THE BACKGROUND EXPANDS THE TAIGA, THE LARGE BOREAL FOREST OF CONIFER TREES.

85 TOP THE BARE ROCKY LANDSCAPE OF THE NATIONAL PARK IS DOMINATED BY CHALLENGING WHICH, THIS TIME, EMERGE FROM A SEA OF CLOUDS.

85 BOTTOM THERE PARK HAS A LARGE NUMBER OF LAKES AND OTHER WET ZONES HOME TO VARIOUS SPECIES OF FISH WELL ADAPTED TO LIVE IN FREEZING WATERS WHICH ARE COVERED FOR THE MOST PART OF THE YEAR BY A LAYER OF ICE.

Olympic National Park
Washington

The park includes the coast and central zone of the Olympic Peninsula that marks the western boundary of the United States. It is a harsh and wild area, with imposing mountain peaks characterized by great glaciers that feed lakes and rivers with torrential currents and freezing waters. On the mountainsides thick forests of Douglas firs grow, trees of monumental dimensions that can reach heights of 250 ft (76 m) – the height of a 25-story building.

Since human intervention in the forests has always been limited – and has become even more limited with the institution of new restrictions – the forests are in their original condition, with winding narrow paths and clearings caused by the fall of colossal trees. Swatches of ferns, lichens, mosses and grasses with intense spring flowering develop in the underbrush. Other species present are the giant Sitka fir and the Western hemlock. The park's temperate rainforests, situated to the northwest, absorb most of the rain that arrives from the Pacific; they are remnants of the rainforest that at one time covered the entire Pacific coast.

Of the park's total extent, 95 percent is considered a wilderness area, and isolation from glaciers and mountains has promoted the well-being of growth of 15 species of indigenous animals, including the United States' largest unmanaged herd of Roosevelt elk in the wild (Olympic was almost named "Elk National Park") and 8 species of indigenous plants, including the avalanche lily, bear grass, violets, and broadleaf lupines.

The park includes 60 miles (96.5 km) of wild Pacific coastline with a population of sea otters, carnivorous mammals perfectly adapted to sea life because of their thick fur, their natural swimming abilities, and their diet based on mollusks, crustaceans and other marine life forms.

There are numerous archaeological sites that contain the remains of Native American settlements: in fact, the Pacific Northwest is the area within the United States that contains the highest number of native populations and tribes. They include the Makah, Hoh, Quileute, and Skokomish tribes whose existence until recent times was intertwined with the wildlife, in a relationship of harmonious usage that never caused the extinction of any species.

The park, which was established in 1938 to protect the Roosevelt deer, became a Biosphere Reserve in 1976 and a Wilderness Area in 1981.

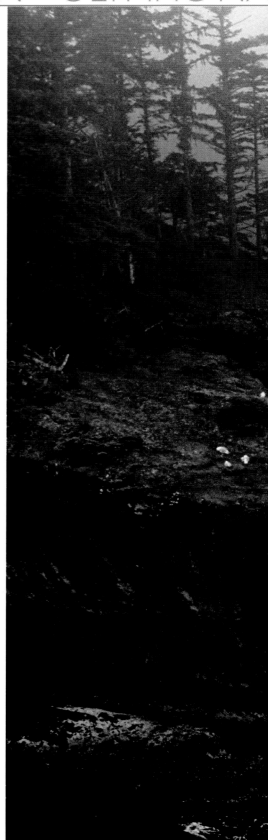

86 THE FIRST SUN RAYS ILLUMINATE A DENSE PINE FOREST WHICH EXTENDS TO THE BEACH.

86-87 FOG SHROUDS THE CAPE FLATTERY FOREST ON THE OLYMPIC PENINSULA. THE CAPE IS THE EXTREME NORTHWEST POINT ON THE PACIFIC COAST WHERE CLIMATIC CONDITIONS ALLOW FOR PLUVIAL VEGETATION.

87 TOP RIGHT A COMMON SEAL RELAXES AT DAWN.

88-89 SEA OTTERS HAD BECOME VERY RARE AT THE END OF THE 19TH CENTURY. THANKS TO TO PROTECTION, THEIR NUMBER HAS INCREASED.

Olympic

90 THE AMERICAN BLACK BEAR IS SMALLER THAN ITS COUSIN, THE GRIZZLY BEAR. UNLIKE THE GRIZZLY, THE BLACK BEAR IS ABLE TO EASILY CLIMB TALLEST TREES.

90-91 TEMPERATE RAINFORESTS DEPEND NOT ONLY ON INTENSE RAINFALLS BUT ALSO ON THE MOISTURE DERIVED FROM THE FOG WHICH, EVERY DAY, DEPOSITS ITSELF ON THE TREE LEAVES.

91 TOP LEFT IT IS RARE FOR A DEER TO GIVE BIRTH TO TWO CALVES WHICH ARE BORN WITH SOFT WHITE SPOTTED FUR THAT ACTS AS PERFECT CAMOUFLAGE IN THE CHIAROSCURO OF THE FOREST.

91 TOP RIGHT MADISON CREEK FALLS, SITUATED IN THE VALLEY OF THE ELWHA RIVER ARE IN HEART OF THE OLYMPIC NATIONAL PARK. THIS PARK IS ONE OF THE WETTEST AREAS IN NORTH AMERICA AND HAS ONE OF THE LARGEST NUMBERS OF STREAMS.

Olympic

92-93 AT THE START OF WINTER, MOUNT ANGELES IS ALREADY COVERED IN A BLANKET OF SNOW WHICH COATS CONIFER FORESTS, PINES, FIRS AND LARCHES.

93 TOP A MOUNTAIN LION CHASES A WHITE HARE WHICH IS ITS MOST FREQUENT PREY, ESPECIALLY DURING WINTER WHEN THE AGILE FELINE, WITH A FEW LONG LEAPS, IS ABLE TO CATCH EVEN THIS SWIFT MOUNTAIN DWELLER.

93 BOTTOM SNOW HAS BY NOW TAKEN POSSESSION OF MOUNTAINS, COATING FORESTS, FIELDS, VALLEYS, AND ROCKY PEAKS. HOWEVER LIFE DOES NOT STOP BECAUSE SEVERAL SPECIES OF ANIMALS SPEND THE WINTER IN THESE MOUNTAINS.

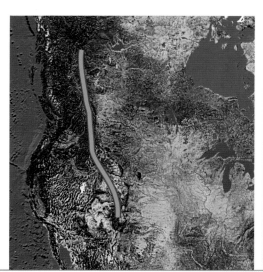

94 TOP CENTER A HORNED OWL HAS BUILT ITS NEST IN THE CAVITY OF A BIG TRUNK.

94 TOP RIGHT CHINESE WALL: THIS IS THE NAME GIVEN TO A BIG ROCKY FORMATION IN THE STATE OF MONTANA.

94-95 NORTH AMERICA'S BACKBONE IS REPRESENTED BY THE ROCKY MOUNTAINS.

ROCKY MOUNTAINS - FROM ALASKA TO NEW MEXICO -

Rocky Mountains
from Alaska to New Mexico

The Rocky Mountains extend along the entire length of North America, from Alaska to Mexico, crossing the states of Montana, Idaho, Wyoming, Utah, Colorado and New Mexico. The central core of the range is formed by crystalline rock with formations of sedimentary rock along the margins. These mountains have been profoundly shaped by glaciations and meteoric erosion and also feature examples of volcanic phenomena. Several protected areas have been established, including the Canadian Rocky Mountain Parks and the Rocky Mountain National Park in the United States, which was founded on the initiative of a group of naturalists and administrators who already feared the destruction of these natural wonders at the end of the 19th century.

The American President Woodrow Wilson signed legislation on January 26, 1915 to create the national park. In 1976 the protected area received recognition through the United Nations' prestigious Man and the Biosphere Program, becoming a Biosphere Reserve, one of the natural areas exemplifying the biodiversity that it is essential to preserve.

Even at the height of summer, the high altitudes and northern faces are home to impressive snowfields, which are renewed by snowfall each autumn and winter. The entire region comprises a series of different habitats, even though more than a third of its total area lies above the timberline.

Consequently, the dominant landscape is that of the tundra, populated by the few grasses, low-growing shrubs, lichens and mosses able to survive the extremely harsh winter conditions. Huge conifer forests characterize the northern region of the range, while the desert zone dominates the western part in the United States.

These mountains are home to much of North America's fauna, including elk, wolves (that are still relatively common in the wilder parts of the range) and the mule deer, which is one of the favorite prey of pumas and wolves. It is also the habitat of black bear and coyote.

95 TOP CALM, BLUE WATERS, FERTILE FIELDS, CONIFER AND DECIDUOUS FORESTS CHARACTERIZE A LARGE PART OF THE ROCKY MOUNTAINS.

95 BOTTOM IN THE PHOTO WE SEE A MALE ELK DURING THE MATING SEASON. THE ELK IS ONE OF THE LARGEST AMERICAN HERBIVORES.

96-97 A FOREST OF BIRCHES, IN THE LIGHT OF DAWN, IS OUTLINED AGAINST THE REDDISH-CAST ROCKS.

97 TOP DECIDUOUS TREES TAKE ON THE COLOR OF FALL: THE POPLARS BECOME PALE YELLOW, THE MAPLE BECOME RED AND THE SHRUBS BECOME ORANGE.

97 BOTTOM THE MOUNTAIN LION IS WIDESPREAD FROM ALASKA TO TIERRA DEL FUEGO.

98-99 THE ROCKY MOUNTAINS REACH A PARTICULARLY IMPOSING HEIGHT IN THE STATE OF ALBERTA, CANADA.

Timeless **North America**

97

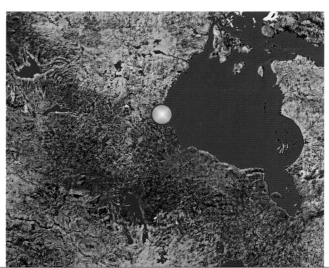

100 TOP LEFT THE COASTLINE APPEARS
SHIFTED BECAUSE OF THE EFFECT OF
WIND CURRENTS AND THE INTENSE
ACTIVITY OF THE ICE.

100-101 AND 101 BOTTOM
TAIGA COVERS A LARGE PART OF
THE NATIONAL PARK.

101 TOP UNLIKE THE EUROPEAN AND
ASIATIC REINDEER, THE CARIBOU HAS
NEVER BEEN DOMESTICATED BY MAN.

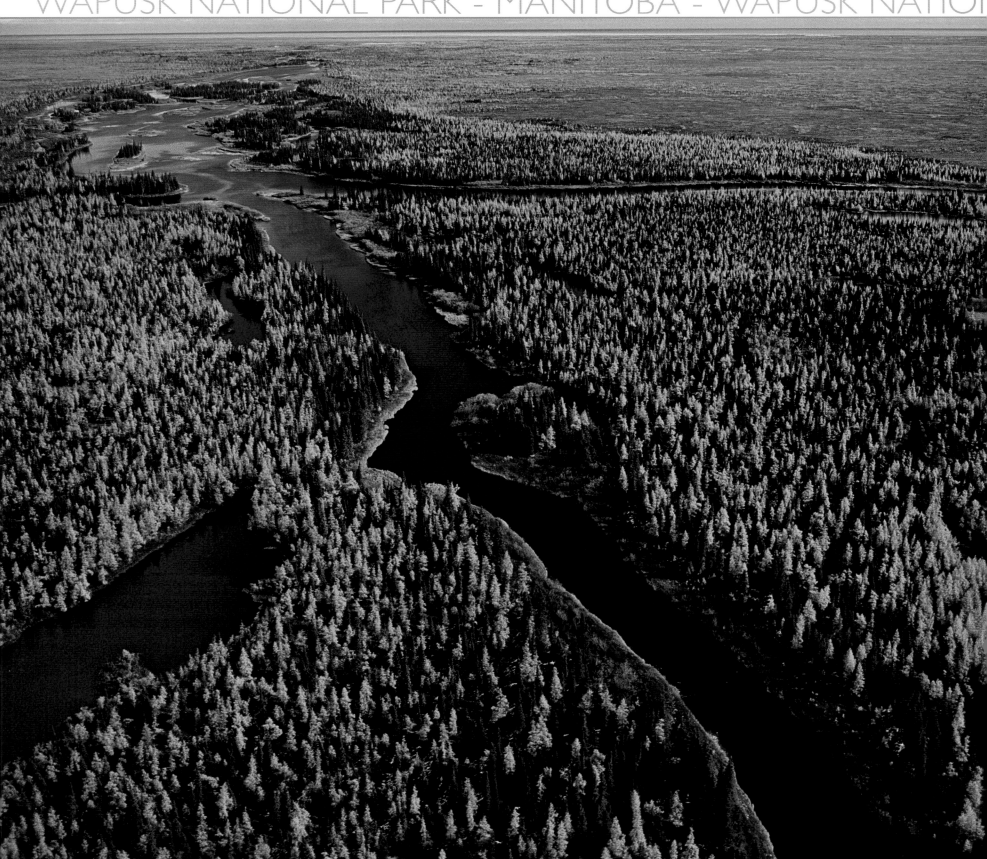

Wapusk National Park
Manitoba

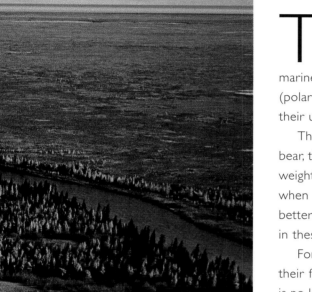

This desolate land, held in the grip of ice for most of the year, has a brief Arctic summer: the ground is free of snow; small plants flower; marine birds attend to their broods; and "white" bears (polar bears) – the great predators – go in search of their usual prey, especially seals.

These islands are the headquarters of the polar bear, the earth's greatest predator. A male can reach a weight of 1325 lbs (600 kg) and a height of 10 ft (3 m) when standing on his hind legs: no other predator is better in terms of strength, skills and the ability to live in these regions, the coldest on Earth.

For centuries man has hunted bears mercilessly for their fur; today they are protected, and their problem is no longer gunshot wounds but contaminants such as PCBs. Borne by marine currents, winds and the food chain, PCBs and other chlororganic compounds – a true "dirty dozen" of poisons – reach the Arctic and accumulate in the bodies of the polar bears, irreversibly altering their development. The Lord of the Arctic who had never known enemies during his frozen reign has been hit hard, and today there are many programs to prevent the extinction of this magnificent predator.

The park covers a vast area of the Hudson-James Lowlands, a flatland that borders Hudson Bay. Extended blankets of permafrost cover this territory, which is geologically rather young: it is in fact slowly rising (about 3 ft/1 m every 100 years), since the ice that covered it started melting, 9000 years ago. This phenomenon, known as isostasis, can be tracked by observing the position of the ancient bank lines along the coast of Hudson Bay.

Archaeology report that the first inhabitants of the area were the Dene and Cree Inuits, who have lived here for more than 3000 years. The first European colonists did not arrive until the 18th century. At about this time, the indigenous populations settled definitively in the present-day location of Prince of Wales Fort and York Factory, now considered National Historical Sites inside the park.

Other unique aspects of the area are the marine coast habitat, characterized by brackish lagoons, sand dunes and beaches, and the presence of tundra and taiga. Water covers about half of the park's surface area, in the form of lakes, rivers and streams.

Animal life is very rich and the park is home to 44 species of mammals, including the polar bear and the caribou. This latter, which form great herds near Cape Churchill, is a prime source of food for the indigenous peoples.

102 TOP A GROUP OF BELUGA
WHALES EMERGES TO BREATH FROM
A SMALL SPACE FREE FROM ICE.
ONLY THROUGH CONSTANT
MOVEMENT CAN THE WHALES
KEEP THE WATER FROM
FREEZING OVER.

102-103 A FEMALE POLAR BEAR
WITH HER TWO QUITE GROWN-UP
CUBS UNDERTAKES THE DIFFICULT
PATH THROUGH ICE WHICH IN
EARLY SUMMER IS STARTING
TO CRUMBLE.

103 TOP ICE TAKES ON DIFFERENT COLORS BECAUSE OF THE PRESENCE OF SEAWEED THAT HAS STUCK BETWEEN THE ICE CRYSTALS.

103 BOTTOM THE AURORA BOREALIS TINGES THE SKY OF WAPUSK PARK IN A COLD GREEN COLOR.

104-105 WALRUSES CAN HANDLE EVEN THE COLDEST SEASONS THANKS TO THE SUBSTANTIAL LAYERS OF FAT WHICH FODDER THEIR BODIES AND INSULATES THEM.

Wapsuk

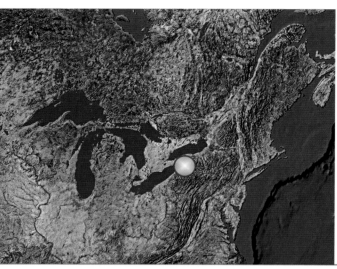

106 TOP RIGHT AND 106-107 WATER PLUNGING OVER HORSESHOE FALLS, SO CALLED BECAUSE OF THEIR SHAPE.

107 TOP WOODED ISLETS STUD THE WATERCOURSE, POUNDED BY FIERCE CURRENTS.

107 BOTTOM THE WATER FLOW OF THE CASCADES INCREASES DRAMATICALLY IN THE SPRING MONTHS.

108-109 MILLIONS OF CUBIC FEET OF WATER CONTINUE TO FALL EVEN DURING WINTER, GIVING RISE TO MISTS.

NIAGARA ESCARPMENT BIOSPHERE RESERVE - ONTARIO -

Niagara Escarpment Biosphere Reserve

Ontario

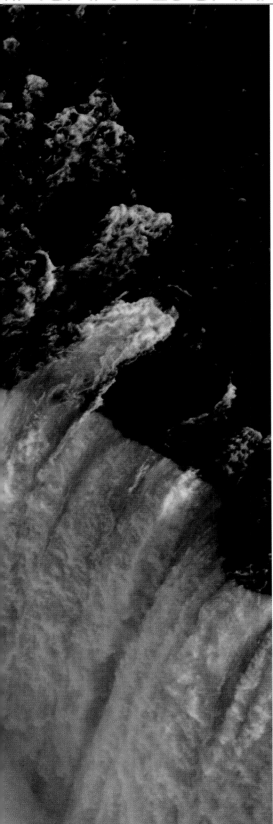

The Niagara Escarpment Biosphere Reserve covers approximately 450 sq. miles (1165 sq. km) extending from Lake Ontario, near the Niagara Falls, to Tobermory, and it forms the structure of the area called Bruce Peninsula, between Georgian Bay and Lake Huron. In geological terms, the "escarpment" is the front of a series of rocky layers that on one side descend slightly and on the other form a drop, a more or less a step.

Water has profoundly modified the reserve's rocky landscape, carving out a series of canyons and then, after a succession of descents, by flowing over an enormous drop that gives rise to the spectacular Niagara Falls, one of the most impressive phenomena of its kind in the world. Most of the protected area is occupied by forest, composed primarily of pine and fir trees in the northern part and by deciduous trees in the south.

The reserve, established in 1990, actually consists of two protected areas: the Bruce Peninsula National Park and the Marine Park of Fathom Five, with a human population of about 120,000 inhabitants spread out over 22 towns. It is therefore a relatively populated area, but no less interesting from a naturalist's standpoint. In fact, aside from the urban and farm areas, the core of the reserve consists of the main and neighboring falls known together as the Niagara Falls, but also of the forests, humid zones and rock walls.

The rock that characterizes this territory, whose formation began approximately 430 million years ago, is essentially very hard dolomite that resists erosion better than the rock strata under it (limestone, sandstone and schist). This causes the breakage of the blocks above, worn away at the bottom by river waters, with the subsequent receding of the falls. The erosion that over the millennia created fantastic gorges and ravines also explains why today the Niagara Falls are situated seven miles upstream from what was once the main front. Other places of note are the steep rock walls, the grottoes and the cavern phenomena (Cyprus Lake, Grotto and Georgian Bay), for which the area is famous.

The rocky inclines of the banks of the Niagara River are flanked by forests of white cedar (Thuya occidentalis); recently a venerable specimen of more than 500 years old was found only one mile from Highway 401. Since then many more have been discovered, even older ones (up to 1000 years old), with the dimensions of a bonsai. Among these was one estimated to be 1845 years old, but unfortunately dead, and only 5 ft (1.5 m) tall as a result of the harsh and difficult environmental conditions under which it grew.

Ferns, lichens and moss cover the other walls of the cliffs, and hundreds of cavities offer shelter to crows, vultures, swallows and bats. It is a wonderful ecosystem, similar to the type called cryptoendolithic ("hidden within the rocks") that describes the community of algae and fungi that live inside the small cavities in the dolomite rock of the cliff.

110 TOP LEFT FORESTS OF DECIDUOUS TREES, ESPECIALLY POPLARS AND WILLOWS, GROW ON THE RIVER BANKS AND, WITH THE LOW TEMPERATURES, THEY GRADUALLY TAKE ON THE WARMER COLORS OF FALL.

110 TOP RIGHT THE RIVER BANKS DISPLAY STRATIFIED ROCKS, OFTEN ERODED BY WEATHERING FACTORS, ESPECIALLY WHERE THE VEGETAL COAT DOES NOT MANAGE TO CONTRIBUTE ITS PROTECTIVE ACTION.

110-111 AROUND THE WATERFALLS EXTENDS THE TYPICAL WOODY LANDSCAPE THAT LINKS THE BOREAL CONIFER FOREST AND THE TEMPERATE DECIDUOUS ONE.

111 TOP IN THE PROTECTED AREA, BESIDE THE PRINCIPAL WATERFALLS, THERE ARE NUMEROUS MINOR STREAMS WHICH GIVE LIFE TO SMALL PONDS DEEP IN THE THICK VEGETATION.

111 BOTTOM DECIDUOUS TREE FORESTS WHICH GROW IN THE AREA OF THE NIAGARA FALLS ARE THE HABITAT OF MANY SPECIES OF MAMMALS AND BIRDS.

Gros Morne National Park
Newfoundland

Situated along Canada's Atlantic coast, which is known for its winter storms and for the dense fog that often covers it, Newfoundland is one of the areas that has contributed most to the progress of the geological knowledge of our world.

Like a big book opened to the history of our planet, the rocks of the Gros Morne National Park illustrate the changes that occurred from the Precambrian period to the present, changes which caused the disappearance of the old ocean plates and the birth of new Continental plates.

Rocks from the Devonian period that emerged in the park area have remained relatively stable, aside from erosion, upheaval, and some slight movement along the main fault lines. In the last two million years, the Glacial and Interglacial Periods, linked to the change of ocean level, produced the area's morphology as it is today. So informative is the terrain and so valuable as a source of geological history that it is wholly understandable that in 1987 UNESCO declared Gros Morne National Park a World Heritage Site. Two different types of landscape dominate the park: the low shorelines on the edges of the Gulf of St. Lawrence and the alpine plateau of the Long Range Mountains. In addition to the beauty of the scenery, which ranges from sandy coasts to mountaintops, and from forests to tundra, there is a great variety of flora and fauna to admire in the park. This results largely from the particular mixture of species typical of the temperate, boreal and arctic zones.

The park has more than 700 species of flowering plants, 400 mosses and worts, more than 400 species of lichens and 239 recorded species of birds, including such summer visitors hermit thrushes, ruby-crowned kinglets, yellow-bellied flycatchers, winter wren, warblers of several types, and the curiously named ovenbird. The oldest human presence in the area dates back to more than 5000 years ago, with the first of the ancient Indian populations that settled here from Labrador (L'Anse Amour is the site of the most ancient burial mounds known in North America). Later, the Paleo-Eskimos settled in this area, hunting marine mammals, especially seals. For sixteen centuries they lived here, leaving no other traces. The term "recent Indian cultures" indicates the occupation of other later populations that replaced the Paleo-Eskimos. Their remains in Gros Morne can be traced back to about a thousand years ago. It was at that time that some Northern European peoples arrived on the Newfoundland coast; the remains of their settlement contained the most ancient European remains in North America. The remains of one Viking settlement, discovered in 1960, are now part of the L'Anse au Meadows National Historical Site.

112 EROSION CAUSED BY GLACIERS
AND WATER CURRENTS UNCOVERS THE
ANCIENT ROCKS CONSTITUTING A LARGE
PART OF THE PARK'S TERRITORY.

112-113 AND 113 TOP LEFT
THE SCENERY OF GROS MORNE
NATIONAL PARK IS DOMINATED BY
VAST FORESTS. THEIR UNIFORMITY
IS INTERRUPTED ONLY BY MARSHES,
LAKES AND ROCK FORMATIONS.

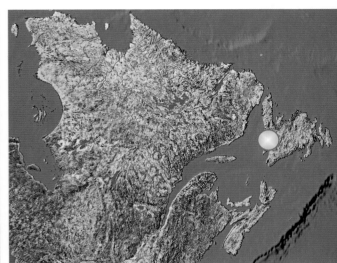

114 TOP THE ATLANTIC PUFFIN IS A SEABIRD FROM THE AUK FAMILY, AND IS DISTANTLY RELATED TO SEAGULLS.

114 CENTER, BOTTOM AND 114-115 THE COAST IS EXTREMELY VARIED, ALTERNATING BETWEEN STEEP ROCKS AND AREAS OF PEBBLY AND SANDY BEACHES. THE GROS MORNE IS FOUND IN A VERY HUMID PART OF CANADA AND, FOR A LARGE PART OF THE YEAR, ITS MOUNTAINS ARE ENVELOPED BY DENSE WHITE CLOUDS OF FOG.

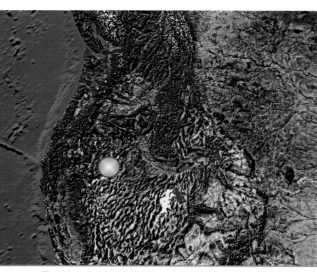

116 TOP RIGHT AND 116-117 THE CALDERA IS A VAST, ALMOST PERFECTLY CIRCULAR, HOLLOW FORM WHICH, PROGRESSIVELY FILLED WITH RAINWATER WITH THE PASSING OF CENTURIES.

117 ONLY PART OF THE STEEP SLOPES WHICH FLANK THE LAKE IS COVERED WITH VEGETATION, THIS IS ALSO DUE TO SNOW WHICH COVERS THE AREA FOR MOST OF THE YEAR.

Crater Lake National Park
Oregon

This national park in the heart of North America was established to protect the landscape, born of a powerful volcanic phenomenon: the collapse of Mount Mazama after a giant eruption about 8000 years ago. The result was a vast cavity, a caldera that with the passing of the centuries progressively filled up with water from rainfall and formed a lake with absolutely unique characteristics.

There are very few aquatic life forms here; fish, for example, could not reach this lake because of the absence of connections to other hydrographic systems: the lake has no effluents or tributaries. It boasts a depth of 2000 ft (6190 m); it is the deepest in the United States and seventh deepest in the world. Its waters are among the purest yet found on earth, allowing the development of plant life even at considerable depths.

This national park was established in 1902; it extends over some 250 sq. miles (650 sq. km), and its primary focus is the preservation of this precious ecosystem, even though it includes the vast forests that grow on the slopes of the ancient volcanic crater. Goshawks, various species of buzzards, numerous birds of prey and woodpeckers live there. The ecosystem hosts numerous land animals, some of modest size like the fox and mustelids such as the marten and also larger ones such as the baribal (back bear), which feeds primarily on berries, grasses, tubers and insects but occasionally hunts deer, which are present in large numbers.

One of the major curiosities of the park, which is now the destination of a substantial number of tourists, is the floating trunk of a colossal tree, a hemlock (Tsuga mertensiana). The trunk has now been floating on the water for more than a century, pushed around by the wind, and has been christened with the nickname "The Old Man."

118 TOP THE GOSHAWK IS ONE OF THE MOST POWERFUL AND SWIFTEST PREDATORS OF THE ZONE. THANKS TO THE SHORT, ROUNDED WINGS AND ITS LONG TAIL, IT IS CAPABLE OF CARRYING OUT RAPID MANEUVERS EVEN IN THE DENSE FORESTS.

118-119 THE LAKE, WHICH IS 1942 FT (592 M DEEP), IS THE DEEPEST OF THE UNITED STATES AND THE SEVENTH DEEPEST IN THE WORLD. ITS WATERS ARE AMONG THE CLEAREST IN THE WORLD.

Crater Lake

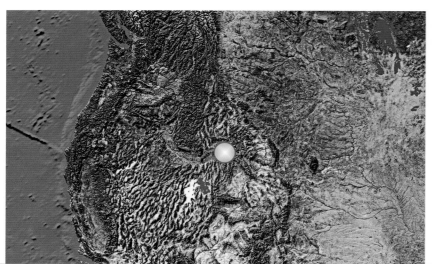

120 TOP RIGHT GEYSERS ARE AMONG THE MOST FAMOUS AND CHARACTERISTIC ELEMENTS OF THE NATIONAL PARK. SOME OF THEM ERUPT WITH A CHRONOMETRICAL REGULARITY AND REACH DOZENS OF FEET OF HEIGHT.

120-121 AND 121 CANYONS EXCAVATED BY THE WATER FLOW, GREAT FORESTS, LAKES, AND VOLCANIC FORMATIONS CONSTITUTE THE SPECTACULAR LANDSCAPE OF YELLOWSTONE NATIONAL PARK.

Yellowstone National Park

Idaho

Yellowstone Park is the park of the great animals of North America: the grizzly and black bears, the elk and bison, American lynxes, the coyotes, otters and beavers. They live in the great forests, along the rivers and in the prairies of this boundless territory. Until recently only one important element was missing to complete the animal picture: the wolf. Long persecuted, it had been gone for a many years, but some decades ago it was decided to reintroduce it. The project came to pass and today an important wolf population, the magnificent predator of North America, has returned to hunt its favorite prey in the seclusion of the father of all national parks.

The park is in fact the world community's first national park. It was established in 1872 to protect the land that so fascinated the pioneers who dedicated their lives to the exploration and conquest of the Far West. Yellowstone is also one of the world's largest protected areas; it extends almost 2.2 million acres (900,000 hectares) in the states of Wyoming, Idaho and Montana.

Yellowstone is also one of the "hottest" spots on Earth; a large outcropping of magmatic material, very close to the surface, gives rise to an impressive and unique series of geological phenomena. The park is also home to an unrivaled cluster of geysers (about 300 in total), the oldest of which, "Old Faithful," has become a symbol of the park and is recognized all over the world. Its attributes have in fact remained substantially unchanged over the past 100 years. The perfect timing of its eruptions and their height of more than 200 ft (61 m) always leave visitors incredulous.

The fossil forest, Yellowstone Lake — one of the largest mountain lakes in the world — and all of the other innumerable and spectacular hydrothermal manifestations (such as the travertine terraces of Mammoth Hot Springs, active for more than 115,000 years in the northern part of the park) continue to attract more than 30,000 visitors a day, a phenomenon that represents quite a challenge for the park administration to manage.

The park was established in 1872 by President Ulysses S. Grant after John Colter, the first white man to travel across the area, spoke of the extraordinary beauty of the place upon his return from an exploratory journey: pools of bubbling mud, stone wells, geysers that spouted water into the air — stories so incredible that for many years he was not believed. Many other expeditions were necessary to confirm Colter's story, the decisive one being that of Ferdinand Hayden, who brought artists and photographers in tow. It was then decided to preserve the place for the spiritual enjoyment of future generations as well. Unknown to whites, but well known among the indigenous people, the area is the fact that Yellowstone was the long home and hunting ground of the Tukudikas people.

Yellowstone has been an International Biosphere Reserve since 1976 and a World Heritage Site since 1978. The southern part of the park borders Grand Teton National Park.

122 TOP THE COYOTE IS ONE OF NORTH AMERICA'S MOST ADAPTABLE SPECIES. IT IS ABLE TO
LIVE A SHORT DISTANCE AWAY FROM HUMANS AND BENEFIT FROM WHAT IS MADE AVAILABLE
BY FARMERS AND TOURISTS.

122 BOTTOM A FEMALE WAPITI WITH HER FOAL. WAPITIS MATE IN THE FALL, CHALLENGING
EACH OTHER IN EXHAUSTING ANTLER FIGHTS.

123 A FEMALE BLACK BEAR PROTECTS ITS CUBS WHICH ARE SHOWING REMARKABLE
TREE-CLIMBING ABILITIES, ESSENTIAL SKILLS TO ESCAPE FROM THEIR WORST ENEMY:
THE GRIZZLY BEAR.

124-125 THE MIDWAY GEYSER BASIN IS CHARACTERIZED BY ITS ALMOST PERFECTLY CIRCULAR
FORM AND ITS EYE-CATCHING COLORATION.

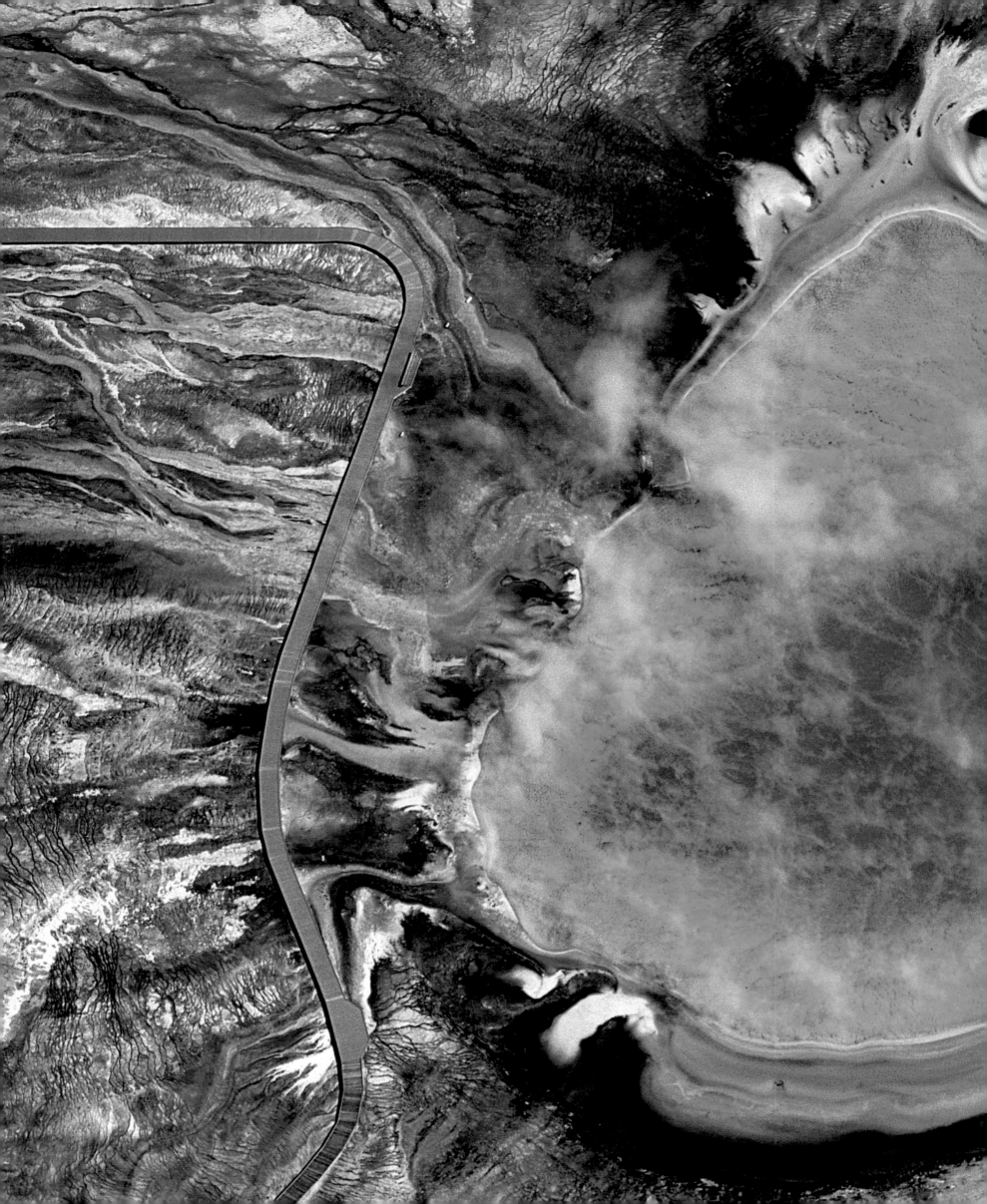

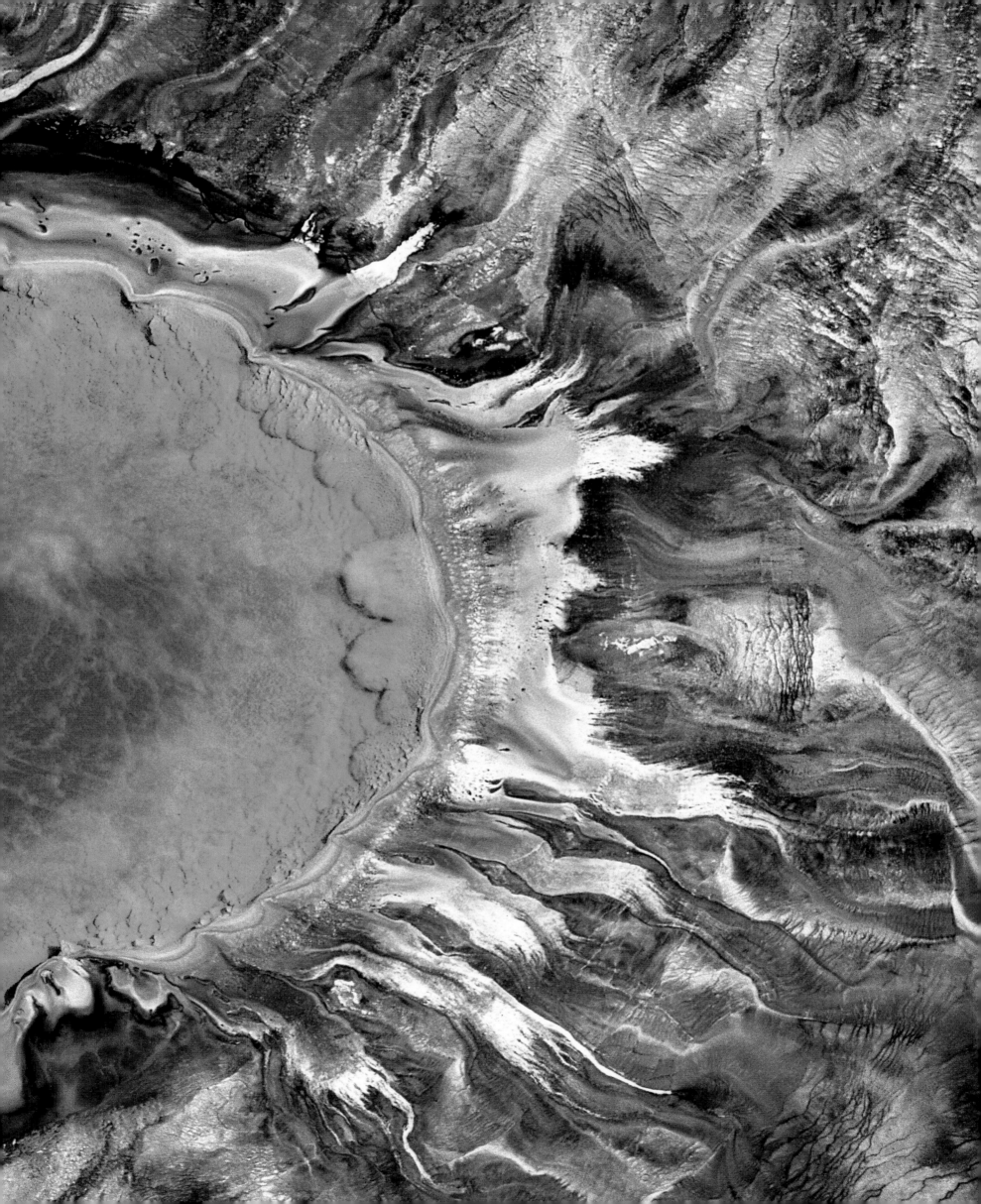

126 TOP THANKS TO A SUCCESSFUL REINTRODUCTION EFFORT, A NOW SIGNIFICANT
POPULATION OF WOLVES HAS RETURNED TO HUNT DEER AND BISON IN THE PARK.

126 BOTTOM THE PARK IS ONE OF THE "WARMEST" PLACES ON EARTH. THIS
IS BECAUSE OF AN IMPOSING RISE OF MAGMATIC MATERIAL, VERY CLOSE TO
THE SURFACE, WHICH GIVES LIFE TO AN IMPRESSIVE AND UNIQUE SERIES
OF GEOLOGIC WONDERS.

127 THE YELLOWSTONE NATIONAL PARK WAS INSTITUTED IN 1872 BY PRESIDENT
ULYSSES GRANT WHO, ALONG WITH SOME OTHER FAR-SIGHTED AMERICANS,
WAS CONCERNED ABOUT THE INCREASING ASSAULTS ON NATURE.

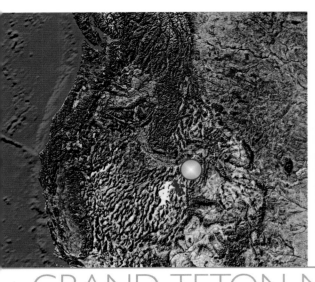

128 TOP ·RIGHT THE ELKS' MATING
SEASON OCCURS IN LATE FALL,
WHEN THE SNOW SEASON STARTS.
MALES CHALLENGE
EACH OTHER IN LONG, EXHAUSTING,
BUT BLOODLESS, DUELS.

128-129 THE PARK INCLUDES A
SPECTACULAR MOUNTAIN RANGE,
ABOUT 50 MILES (80 KM) LONG,
CHARACTERIZED BY TWELVE GRANITE
PEAKS MOST OVER 11,800 FT (3600 M)
IN HEIGHT.

129 GLACIERS AND SNOWFIELDS COVER
THE NUMEROUS LAKES IN THE PARK.

Grand Teton National Park
Wyoming

The Rocky Mountains, the long mountain range that runs like a spine through North America from Alaska to beyond Mexico, include the United States' great national parks. They in turn include terrain that in some areas, like the terrain of the Great North, is defined as wilderness: that is, lacking any tangible signs of human life.

Grand Teton Park, established in 1926 in northern Wyoming, is one of these wilderness areas, along with Yellowstone, the Grand Canyon and Bryce Canyon. It is a park that includes a spectacular mountain range 50 miles (80 km) long, characterized by twelve hard peaks of granite, eight of which are higher than 12,000 feet (3657 m). Grand Teton, the highest mountain, is almost 13,770 feet (4197 m).

The signs left by glaciers are very evident: large glacial cirques, long moraines, and deposits of erratic masses are evidence of the thousands of years of erosion produced by rivers of ice fed every year by copious snowfall. Glaciers and snow then fed numerous lakes, even moraine lakes, and innumerable streams of torrential flow that created magnificent waterfalls.

Jackson Hole Valley, inside the mountain range, and the entire area of the park are the coldest zones in the United States, where harsh, snowy winters seem reluctant to give way to brief and temperate springs and summer. During these seasons the woods become shadowy temples and the life of the small animals of the forest have moments of frenzy: squirrels, weasels, skunks, foxes and hundreds of species of birds run into each other, moving between colossal conifers and deciduous trees. The prairies become covered with blossoms of the many species of wildflowers, and become the showplace of the great grouse and the hunting grounds for the red-tailed buzzard.

The park is the habitat of many species of herbivores — moose, mule deer and elk — which are hunted by the large predators such as the grizzly bear, the wolf, and the coyote.

130 TOP THE PARK'S HIGHEST PEAK IS ALMOST 13,800 FT (4200 M) AND THERE ARE NUMEROUS OTHERS TOP 11,800 FT (3600 M) WITH LARGE GLACIERS, GLACIER VALLEYS, LONG MORAINES, DEPOSITS OF FALLEN BOULDERS.

130-131 MOUNT MORAN DOMINATES OVER JACKSON LAKE IN THE HEART OF THE NATIONAL PARK WHICH WAS CREATED TO PROTECT ONE OF THE MOST STRIKING LANDMARKS OF THE ROCKY MOUNTAINS.

131 TOP BISON ROAM IN SMALL HERDS IN THE FLATTEST PARTS OF THE PARK WHERE THEY FEED ON THE ABUNDANT VEGETATION AVAILABLE.

131 BOTTOM THE GRAN TETON NATIONAL PARK REPRESENTS ONE OF THE MAIN WILDERNESS AREAS OF NORTH AMERICA: IT IS MOSTLY DEVOID OF ANY SIGN OF HUMAN PRESENCE.

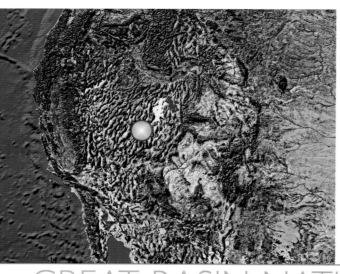

132 TOP RIGHT WHEELER PEAK IS THE SECOND HIGHEST PEAK IN NEVADA.

132-133 THE DESERT ENVIRONMENT OF THE GREAT BASIN IS SURROUNDED BY THE SCHELL CREEK RANGE.

133 TOP THE MOUNTAINS OF THIS PARK RISE ABRUPTLY FROM THE DESERT.

133 BOTTOM THE GOLDEN EAGLE IS ONE OF THE LARGEST BIRD OF PREY. IT LIVES IN THE MOST ISOLATED PARTS OF THE MOUNTAINS AND IS CONSIDERED TO BE PROTECTED SPECIES.

Great Basin National Park

Nevada

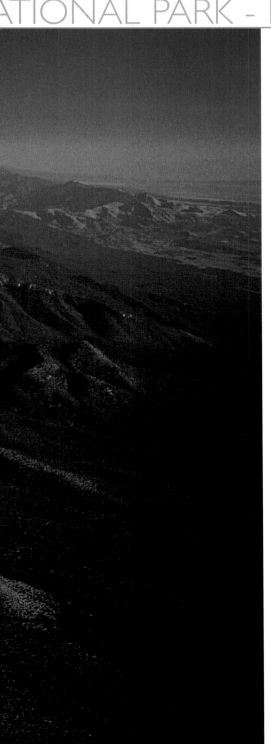

This huge park, established in 1986 is situated on the Nevada-Utah border and occupies part of the vast Great Basin plateau that comprises almost the entire state of Nevada. The Great Basin is bordered by the Sierra Nevada to the west, the Columbia Mountains range to the north, the Rocky Mountains and Colorado plateau to the east, and by Death Valley to the southwest.

The geological history and morphology of the district is particularly interesting. It is true basin, at an average altitude of 4925 ft (1500 m), with no outflow to the sea. Within its borders are various mountain ranges oriented north to south, approximately 62 miles (100 km) long, altered again and again by erosion and by orogenic movement. The ranges enclose hundreds of internal drainage basins, generally comparable to lakes (saline to various degrees) into which rivers such as the Humboldt and Carson flow. The climate is very dry and rainfall does not exceed 10 inches (25 cm) per year, since the clouds stopped by the mountain ranges deposit rain in the area outside of the basin. Because of the aridness of the climate, vegetation is typical of steppes and cold deserts.

The area, having remained isolated for so a long time, is rich in animal and plant species; these differ in some cases from forms present in other territories primarily covered by small mountain ranges, where arid zones give way to alpine pastures.

As a result of its challenging environmental characteristics, the basin was not hospitable to human habitation, though remains have been found of an Indian population that date back to approximately 10,000 years ago. Over a century ago, the discovery of enormous mineral resources (gold, silver, tungsten) led to a sudden increase in the numbers of Americans and European immigrants.

Mining coexisted well with cattle ranching, the principal occupation of the inhabitants of Nevada. Among the park's best-known natural wonders is the Lexington Arch, in the canyon of the same name, a natural arch carved out of limestone. It also hosts one of the oldest trees in the world, a *Pinus longaeva*, named "Prometheus" and dated at 4900 years of age. It was trimmed, still alive, in 1964. Other examples of this species, living and not, are found in the area of Wheeler Peak, the second highest peak in Nevada at 13,063 ft (3981 m) and the United Sates' southernmost glacier, flowing over United moraines of glacial origin. The area was declared a National Monument in 1922.

Great Basin

134 THIS AREA OF THE GREAT BASIN PARK IS CHARACTERIZED BY THE ARIDITY OF THE TERRAIN WHERE A LAKE ONCE EXISTED. IT DRIED UP BECAUSE OF THE SCARCITY OF RAIN.

134-135 WALKER LAKE AND MOUNT GRANT APPEAR ON THE BACKGROUND OF THE SANDY DESERT. MOUNT GRANT FORMS PART OF THE WASSUK MOUNTAIN RANGE.

135 TOP LEFT THE RINGTAIL LIVES MOSTLY IN THE SOUTHWESTERN UNITED STATES.

135 TOP RIGHT THE VEGETATION IS OFTEN SIMILAR TO THAT OF THE STEPPES AND IN THE COLD DESERTS.

136-137 THE LEHMAN CAVES ARE CHARACTERIZED BY RARE ROCKY FORMATIONS.

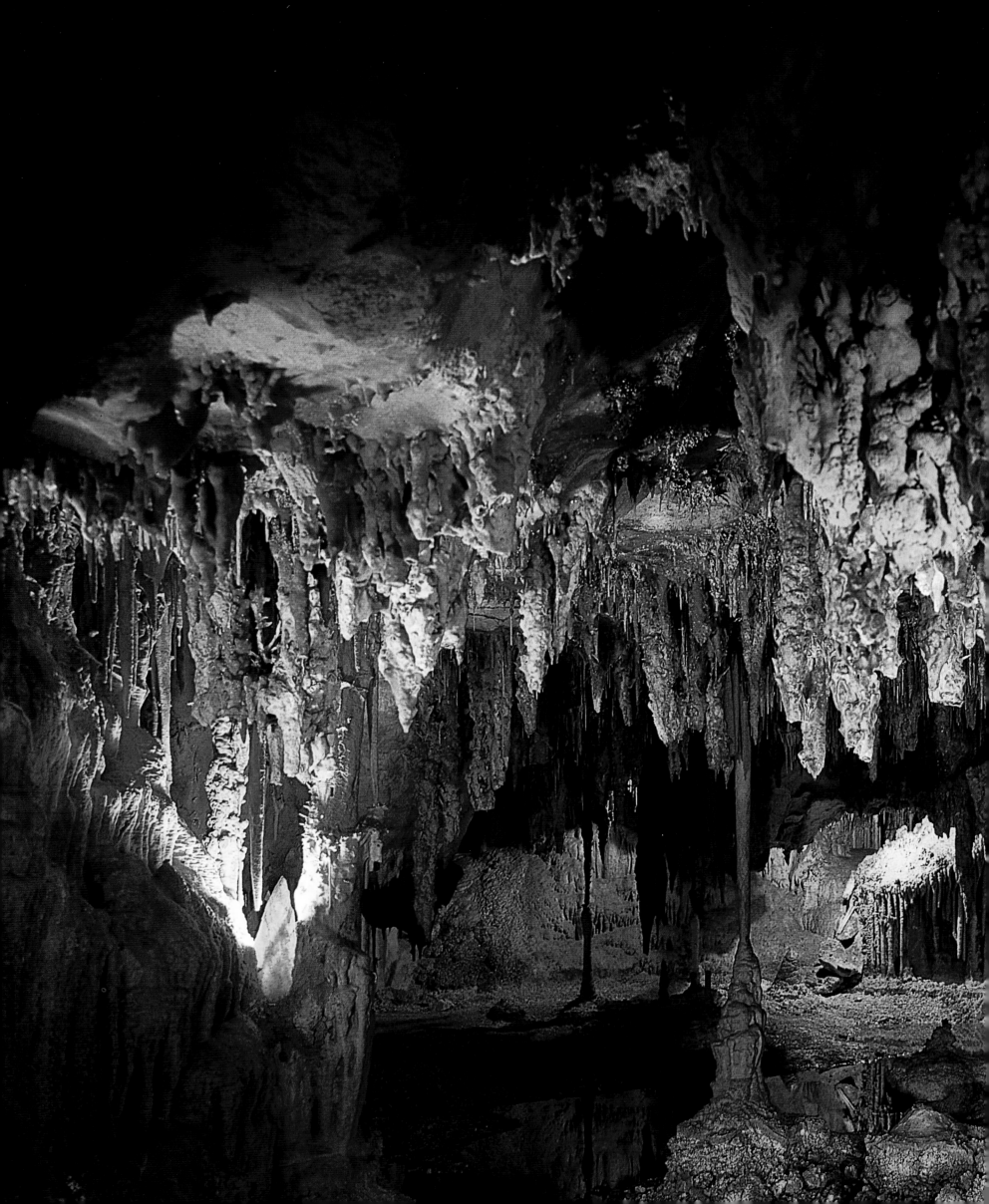

138 TOP AND 138-139 THE HEART OF THE PARK IS REPRESENTED BY A LABYRINTH OF CANYONS WHICH EXTEND FOR ALMOST 22 MILES (35 KM).

139 BOTTOM THE PARK WAS INSTITUTED IN 1926 ESSENTIALLY TO PROTECT THE LANDSCAPE AND GEOLOGICAL FORMATIONS.

140-141, 142-143 AND 144-145 THE FIRST SNOWFALLS OFFER A SPECTACULAR FAIRYTALE APPEARANCE TO THE BRYCE CANYON LANDSCAPE.

Bryce Canyon National Park

Utah

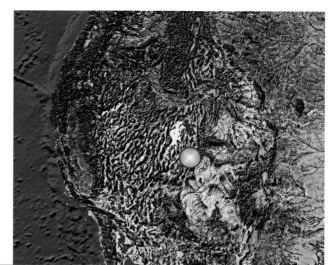

The canyon is named after a Mormon pioneer, Ebenezer Bryce. He lived for a long time in this region of the Rocky Mountains that, like a great book, opens to the geological history of this American region, which often without cover of vegetation shows the various layers of sedimentary rock that were deposited over the course of millions of years.

External agents, especially rain, rivers and wind, worked for a long time like skilled sculptors to create an absolutely unique landscape, with pinnacles, columns, steep cliff walls that plummet down for tens and hundreds of feet and arches shaped so regularly and perfectly that they seem the work of man. Bryce Canyon National Park (37,277 acres/15,085 hectares) is located in southwestern Utah and was established in 1926 especially to protect the land and its geological formations. It is formed by a maze of canyons that extend over almost 22 miles (35 km) along the eastern border of the Paunsaugunt Plateau, composed primarily of schist, sandstone and limestone. Vegetation grows on only scattered parts of the challenging rock, extending in various compositions and patterns governed by altitude and the exposure of the slopes. In some areas, woods of junipers predominate, junipers that live for hundreds of years and achieve colossal dimensions; in others, forests extend that are composed of pine trees that are able to grow in even the steepest areas, outlining the jagged crests.

Birds dominate the wildlife; at least 100 different species are to be found. Among them are nutcrackers, finches, many woodpeckers and raptors. It is easy to hear the woodpeckers with their characteristic pecking on the tree trunks in eager search for insects, and the soaring flight of the raptors are a noble sight. The flight of red-tailed buzzard, the turkey vulture, and the golden eagle is slow and circular, that of falcons and hawks is quick and darting.

The park offers important traces left by the forebears of the Pueblo and Paiute Indians who have lived a long time in the area, building their homes in the rocks.

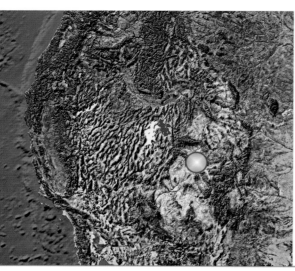

146 TOP RIGHT ANGEL ARCH, IS FOUND IN THE CENTER OF THE NATIONAL PARK.

146-147 ARCHES NATIONAL PARK CONTAINS OVER TWO THOUSAND OF THESE FANTASTIC SCULPTURES.

147 DELICATE ARCH (TOP) IS PERHAPS THE MOST FAMOUS OF THE PARK, (BOTTOM) DRUID ARCH.

Arches National Park

Utah

Between the Colorado River and the Glen River, in a desert region of Utah, is Arches National Park, striking in its wealth of geological phenomena and the intense colors of the rocks that display all shades of red, yellow and brown.

The climate of the area is decidedly continental arid: rain is very limited, temperatures vary greatly with freezing winters and torrid summers, and at night fall dramatically. The region's wildlife has therefore adapted to particular patterns of existence: many of the bird species are migratory; the mammals and reptiles are generally nocturnal, and fall into deep hibernation during the winter season.

Arches National Park, which extends over 76,519 acres (30,966 hectares), is inhabited not only by the biggest and most impressive mammals of North America such as the bear, deer, and coyote, but also by numerous species of reptiles, among which are rattlesnakes, which possess powerful toxins and highly effective sensory systems for locating prey by detecting their heat radiation.

The park's soil is formed by a very thin black crust, which sustains the life of a varied flora including lichens, ferns, and algae.

This park is famous for the natural arches that give it its name; it boasts the world's largest concentration of these wind-eroded natural forms. They total more than two thousand, and among them is the famous "Delicate Arch" of truly graceful proportions.

Other distinctive shapes, created from the thousands of years of weather and water erosion in this area, are the windows and holes carved out at various heights in the rock walls: the pinnacles, monoliths, columns and hoodoos (the name given to what is left of the walls of a "window" in the rock), which are truly natural sculptures.

The park was established in 1971 even though the area had been protected since 1929 through the institution of a link with the pre-existing National Monu-

ment area. It is also known for the abundance of "pots," cavities in the rock that collect the scarce rainwater and sediment carried by the wind. They are home to organisms also able to survive for long periods in the absence of water; they are highly adapted to a life in a state of extreme dehydration. They play an integral role in the food chain of insects, amphibians, reptiles, and other small animals.

Of great interest to anthropologists and archaeologists are the traces in the park of hunters from the Ice Age; they date back to more than 10,000 years ago and confirm very early settlement of the area.

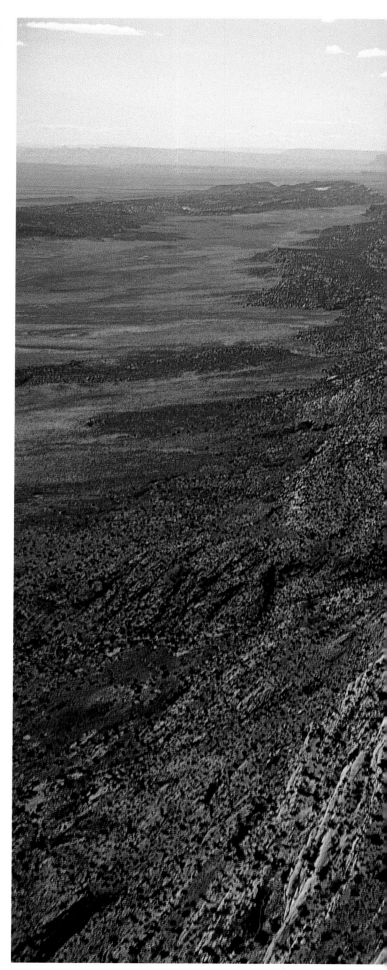

Arches

148 TOP TWO ARCHES APPEAR IN THE
RED SEDIMENTARY ROCK, WHICH SHOWS
A SERIES OF DIFFERENT GEOLOGICAL
LAYERS STRATIFIED ON EACH OTHER.

148 BOTTOM THE DELICATE ARCH ZONE IS
VERY DRY AND IS ALMOST WITHOUT
VEGETATION, WHEREAS THE MOUNTAINS IN
THE BACKGROUND ARE TREE-CLAD.

148-149 THE DEVIL'S GARDEN IS A STRIP
OF SHARP ROCK, HEAVILY ERODED,
ALMOST OR COMPLETELY BARE OF ANY
KIND OF VEGETATION.

150 TOP LAYERS UPON LAYERS OF SEDIMENTARY ROCKS, SHAPED BY THE POWER OF THE EARTH, RISE HIGH, FIGHTING A DAILY BATTLE AGAINST WIND, RAIN AND THE COLD WHICH, LITTLE BY LITTLE, SOFTEN THEIR CONTOURS.

150 BOTTOM IN THE LOW AND WARM LIGHTS OF DUSK, SHADOWS GROW LONGER, CREATING FANTASTIC DRAWINGS ON THE INCREASINGLY RED ROCK.

150-151 WEATHERING FACTORS LIKE WIND, RAIN AND ICE ARE NATURE'S GREAT SCULPTORS, ABLE TO CREATE FANTASTIC WORKS OF ART.

151 TOP LEFT A SPARSE VEGETATION OF BUSHES, ABLE TO RESIST LONG PERIODS OF DRYNESS, MAKES ITS WAY AT THE BOTTOM OF THE CANYON.

151 TOP RIGHT A SERIES OF ARCHES GUARDS ONE OF THE NATIONAL PARK'S REMOTEST AREAS WHERE, IN A DISTANT ICE AGE, COMMUNITIES OF MEN HUNTERS HAD FOUND REFUGE.

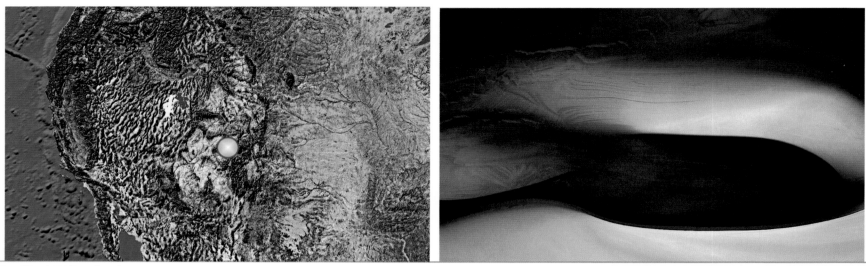

Great Sand Dunes National Park
Colorado

During the Pleistocene Epoch, when glaciers occupied most of the San Luis Valley, sand dunes began to form in this vast protected area in Colorado. The wind slowly accumulated the grains of sand, fruit of the disintegration of rocks, giving birth to a fantastic world of varied hills in a constant state of change, only partially colonized by vegetation that only in some cases becomes particularly thick.

The sand dunes give life to a complex ecosystem with lakes and temporary and permanent pools rich with indigenous and endangered species. Here, in fact, in the Medano and Sand Creek Rivers, the peculiar phenomenon known as "water surges" can be observed. At regular intervals a stream of water forms that flows downstream for a few moments before stopping again. After about 15 seconds the stream flows again, and this continues with extreme regularity; the gush of water is created because small dunes form a barrier to the water, which accumulates behind it. Soon the volume of dammed water increases enough that it flows over the dune and runs downstream.

The Medano and Sand Creek Rivers, fed by the melting of the snows that fall every winter on the highest peaks, are of particular interest for the presence of underwater dunes that result from from the accumulation of sand carried by the current.

The Great Sand Dunes National Park is one of the United States' youngest protected areas, established by President Bill Clinton in 2000 to better protect the National Monument established some 10 years previously to conserve the land threatened by mining that intensified with the discovery of gold. The park also includes the Sangre de Cristo wilderness area and the Sand Creek and Medano Creek catchment basins. The overall area, approaching 85,000 acres (34,400 hectares), is partially managed by the Forest Service as part of the Forests of the Rio Grande.

The fauna includes many species of birds, including woodpeckers, jays, vultures, buzzards, hawks and owls. Among the mammals are martens such as skunks, and canines such as the coyote.

152 TOP RIGHT AND 152-153 THE WIND CONTINUOUSLY BLOWS AWAY SAND ORIGINATING FROM THE DISINTEGRATION OF ROCKS, THUS PRODUCING A FANTASTIC WORLD OF EVER-CHANGING HILLS.

153 AND 154-155 DUNES GIVE LIFE TO A COMPLEX ECOSYSTEM IN WHICH THERE IS A VARIETY OF TREES, PLANT LIFE, AND BUSHES.

156-157 SANDY DUNES STARTED TO FORM IN THE PLEISTOCENE ERA WHEN GLACIERS OCCUPIED MOST OF THE SAN LUIS VALLEY.

Death Valley National Park
California

Death Valley is one of the most inhospitable places on the planet, but is also one of the most spectacular. It only takes looking out on the panoramic Dante's View to understand the idea the American people have of Dante's *Inferno*.

Here daily life must deal with great heat, severe temperature drops at night, ranges, and the almost total lack of water. A small number of plant species are able to flourish – they accumulate water in their trunks and in their roots – but very few animals are able to survive among the rocks

and sand, and most of these are gifted with some of the deadliest poisons invented by nature. It is the only chance that rattlesnakes and scorpions have for survival. Death Valley is situated in the northern part of the Mojave Desert, bordering on Nevada, and is one of the hottest places in the United States; a temperature of 135° F (57° C) in the shade was recorded in July 1913). In form it is a depression running for about 150 miles (240 km) north to south, flanked by the Amargosa and Panamint mountain ranges, which have peaks of over 10,000 feet (3050 m). Within the park is Badwater Basin, which, at 280 ft (85 m) below sea level, is the lowest point in the entire Western Hemisphere. It is so named because the water it holds has a very high salt content. Given these and other feature, it is highly understandable that Death Valley is a true paradise for geology buffs. Notable among the few oases and fresh water springs is Furnace Creek, frequented by the Native Americans and later by gold prospectors. The waters of Salt Creek are home to the pupfish *(Cyprinodon salinus)*, a fish that is able to survive in water that is almost four times more saline than the ocean at a temperature of 110° F (43° C). However, the pupfish is at risk of becoming extinct.

At the end of the 1800s, prospectors found borax in Death Valley; the substance is used in the manufacture of glass, an industry to which the Borax Museum is dedicated. The general manager of the borax mines gave the name Zabriskie Point – later immortalized by Italian director Michelangelo Antonioni in one of his most famous films – to a site from which the visitor can enjoy the panorama of the Golden Canyon. It is also worth noting that the western part of the park occupied by an extensive system of sand dunes that are continually shaped by the wind and tend to assume a typical half-moon shape. Death Valley was declared to be a National Monument in 1933; in 1984 it was designated as a Biosphere Reserve; and in 1994 about 95 percent of the park was declared to be a Wilderness Area. In that same year, the entire Death Valley area of 1.2 million acres (485,620 hectares) was designated a national park.

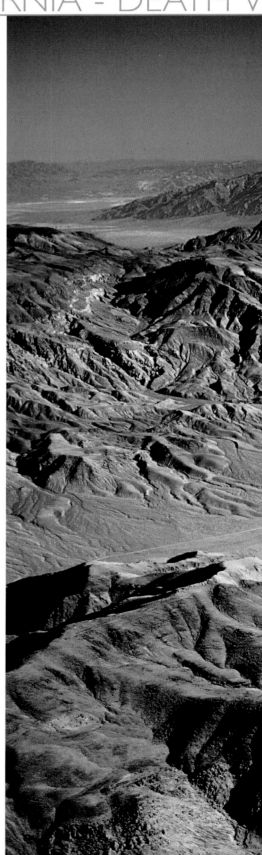

158 TOP THE BADWATER BASIN IS
SITUATED AT ABOUT 262 FT (80 M)
BELOW SEA LEVEL AND IS A TORRID
AND INHOSPITABLE ZONE FOR
ALMOST ALL LIFE FORMS.

158 BOTTOM THE FLAT PARTS OF THE
PARK CONSIST OF SALINE DEPOSITS,
SANDY DUNES AND DRIED-UP BASINS.

158-159 AND 159 TOP LEFT HAVING
HAD SEVERAL WESTERN MOVIES FILMED
IN IT, DEATH VALLEY HAS BECOME THE
MOST FAMOUS NATIONAL PARK IN
THE WORLD

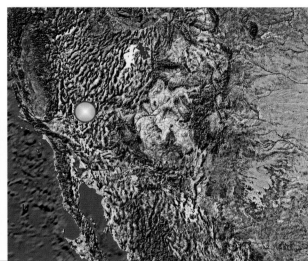

LEY NATIONAL PARK - CALIFORNIA - DEATH VALLEY NATIO

160 TOP MUD DRYING UNDER THE RELENTLESS SUN BEGINS TO CRACK UNTIL IT FORMS STRIKING MOSAICS WHICH EXTEND FOR DOZENS OF MILES.

160-161 SAND DUNES ARE VERY CHANGEABLE, CONTINUOUSLY MODIFIED AND STIRRED BY THE SWEEPING WINDS, THUS MAKING IT IMPOSSIBLE FOR VEGETATION TO GROW.

161 TOP DIFFERENT TYPES OF MINERAL DEPOSITS GIVE THE ROCKS A WIDE VARIETY OF COLORS. THEY VARY FROM CLEAR WHITE BECAUSE OF THE PRESENCE OF SULFUR TO BROWN OR BLACK BECAUSE OF OXIDES.

161 BOTTOM DUNES ARE EVER-CHANGING SANDY WORLDS THAT, BECAUSE OF THE WIND, GAIN THE ELEGANCE OF WORKS CREATED BY A IMAGINATIVE ARCHITECT.

162-163 IN SUMMER, TEMPERATURES SOAR AND, FOR SEVERAL MONTHS, THERE ARE NO RAINFALLS. IN WINTER, HOWEVER, TEMPERATURES PLUNGE DRASTICALLY, OFTEN TO BELOW ZERO.

Sequoia and Kings Canyon National Parks

California

Sharp-ridged mountains, steep, rocky and often inaccessible canyons and million-year-old giant trees: these are the typical elements of the Sierra Nevada, which includes some of North America's highest peaks. Here two parks were established side by side – though at different times – and are now combined as one park of 863,700 acres (350,000 hectares). It protects one of the nation's largest areas of sequoia forests (with four of America's five tallest trees), glacial lands, and waterways that have carved out rocky gorges. Along the

eastern border, outlined against the horizon, is one of the highest mountains in North America, Mount Whitney (14,505 ft/4421 m) dedicated to geologist Josiah Whitney who, in 1873, became the first man to have reached its summit. Also located in this area is Kings Canyon, a wide glacial valley that abruptly narrows to become the deepest canyon in North America.

The park offers equally dramatic geological features below its surface. There, where located in the marble rock, is an immense group of caverns (more than 200 now identified), among which is California's longest grotto, Lilburn Cave. To date more than 15 miles (24 km) of its total length have been explored.

The park's environments are extremely diverse: they range from a rich series of subterranean features through lower altitude terrain, home to typical underbrush and chaparral (a type of bush), up to typical glacial alpine land characteristic of high mountains. For this reason, the variety of plant and animal species and ecosystems is one of the park's most valuable features.

This area is famous for the sequoias, trees of ancient origin considered to be true living fossils. There is an entire forest of them – the Giant Forest – in the southern part of the park, but most noteworthy are the single examples immortalized in photographs and documentaries. General Sherman's Tree is held to be the largest on earth: 276 ft (84 m) high, 36 ft (10.9 m) in diameter at the base.

Somewhat smaller is General Grant's Tree, the third tallest in the state, also known as "The Christmas Tree of the Nation." Moro Rock is one of the most panoramic spots of the park, a great block of granite which offers an exceptional view of the Sierra Nevada and its central valley.

The Sequoia National Park, established in 1890, was the nation's second park; a week later the General Grant National Park was established, along with Yosemite National Park; Kings Canyon National Park was established in 1940.

164 TOP THE PALISADES MOUNTAINS
ARE THE MOST INTACT PART
OF THE REGION.

164 BOTTOM THE PROFILE OF THE
JAGGED CRESTS IS REFLECTED IN
A CALM ALPINE LAKE.

164-165 MOUNT WHITNEY'S SHARP
AND IMPOSING PEAK DOMINATES
SEQUOIA NATIONAL PARK.

165 TOP RIGHT IN KINGS CANYON
NATIONAL PARK, THE STRIATED ROCK
GIVES EVIDENCE OF THE VARIOUS LAYERS
OF DIFFERENT GEOLOGICAL NATURE.

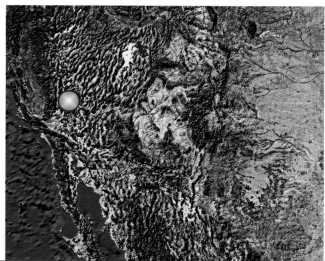

166 GENERAL SHERMAN IS ONE OF THE MOST FAMOUS TREES IN THE WORLD.

167 TOP THE SEQUOIAS ARE LONG-LIVING TREES WHICH CAN SURVIVE FOR TEN CENTURIES, BUT ARE CONSIDERED ANCIENT PLANTS ESPECIALLY IN AN EVOLUTIONARY POINT OF VIEW.

167 CENTER SHAFTS OF LIGHT COLOR ONE OF THE NATIONAL PARK'S WATERFALLS.

167 BOTTOM IN THIS PHOTO, THE BURNT TRUNK OF A LARGE TREE SEEMS TO BE ALMOST ENFOLDED BY THE LIVING AND VITAL TRUNK OF A YOUNGER SPECIMEN.

168-169 THE PRESENCE OF YOUNG TREES IS AN INDICATION OF WELL-BEING OF THE FOREST ECOSYSTEM.

170-171 MOUNT RUSSELL AND MOUNT WHITNEY ARE AMONG THE MOST IMPOSING PEAKS OF THE REGION.

Big Sur Region State Parks
California

172 AND 172-173 ONLY THE FLATTEST LANDS ARE CULTIVATED. A TYPE OF VEGETATION, CALLED THE CHAPARRAL, WHICH RESEMBLES THE MAQUIS (MACCHIA) OF THE MEDITERRANEAN REGION, DOMINATES THE REST OF THE ROCKY TERRITORY.

173 TOP LEFT FOG IS A RECURRING ELEMENT IN THE LANDSCAPE OF THE CALIFORNIAN COAST. DENSE BANKS ARE FORMED ON THE OCEAN AND ARE THEN DRIVEN BY THE BREEZE TOWARDS THE COAST, WHERE THEY BRING PRECIOUS HUMIDITY.

The beaches of California are well known for their vastness, and for a unique ecosystem born of the contact between the Pacific Ocean, more often tempestuous than pacific, and the large mountainous areas of the coastline, often rolling and open but just as often tree-clad. The coast is a world made famous by numerous films and documentaries, a world where millions of seabirds congregate during migration and where there are colonies of sea otters and sea lions dedicated to the capture of their prey in forests of kelp, the large marine algae of the genus *Laminaria*.

Big Sur is a stretch of this fabled coastline extending for about 80 miles (130 km) from Carmel, south of San Francisco, to San Simeon, north of Los Angeles. The region's name derives from from *El Pais Grande del Sur* ("The Great Country of the South") and was bestowed upon it by the Spanish in the 19th century. It has long been recognized as one of the most beautiful stretches of the Californian coast. The renowned and very scenic Highway 1 runs along through the entire Big Sur coast, looking out over rocky cliffs and windswept beaches, almost completely without buildings or other signs of man.

Today the region is safeguarded by a series of protected areas (Point Lobos, Andrew Molera, Pfeiffer Big Sur, Julia Pfeiffer Burns and others). These are connected to other state parks in the area of Monterey to the north and Morro Bay to the south.

These protected areas are easily accessible from the road and offer a great variety of environments: one can find deep, rocky canyons carved out by the torrential currents of the rivers that form charming waterfalls; barren, rocky slopes; and dense forests of deciduous trees and conifers, among which is the Monterey cypress that grows primarily in the Point Lobos area.

Animal species abound, including deer and the fox and otter, but particularly surprising is the variety of birds that come together in large colonies to nest. The sea is especially rich in both large species and small life forms because of the consistent California current, a factor the favors the presence of whales and other migrating cetaceans.

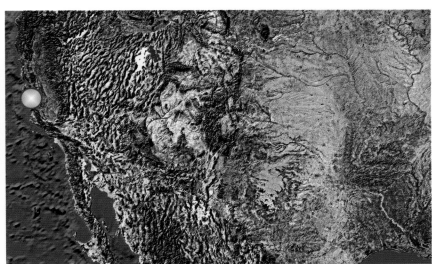

174-175 THE PACIFIC OCEAN ROLLS UP
ONTO THE CALIFORNIAN BEACHES
WHICH ARE WELL KNOWN FOR THEIR
VASTNESS AND FOR THE VARIETY OF
THEIR LANDSCAPES, SOMETIMES ROCKY
AND SOMETIMES SANDY.

175 THE BIG SUR COAST IS THE POINT
OF CONTACT BETWEEN THE PACIFIC
OCEAN, WHICH IS MORE OFTEN
STORMY THAN CALM, AND THE
OFTEN BARREN, MOUNTAINOUS
REGION OF THE HINTERLANDS.

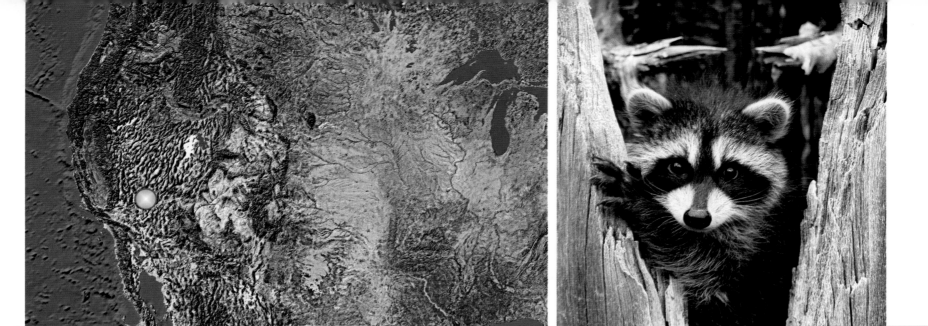

Yosemite National Park
California

The redness of the rocks, the deep blue of a generally serene sky, the dark green of the conifers are the memorable colors of Yosemite National Park, a true monument to nature visited by millions of people every year.

The park is located in the Sierra Nevada, a mountain range in mid-eastern California. The range is of relatively recent origin, formed approximately 3 million years ago due to the rising of an enormous magmatic mass that caused the upheaval of the entire area. The rocky territory has been profoundly modeled by external agents that gave rise to fantastic rocky creations, like the Half Dome, one of the park's most famous symbols, immortalized in the photographs of Ansel Adams. It is a peak 8900 ft (2712 m) high, that approximately 15,000 years ago was divided in two by glaciers that eroded the rock and transported masses of sediment to the valley. Also noteworthy are Yosemite Falls, at 2430 ft (760 m) the highest waterfalls in North America, as well as Glacier Point and Tunnel View, from which the visitor can enjoy the park's finest vistas, and the enormous mass of El Capitan, one of the world's largest outcrops of granite.

The park was established not only to protect the land, but also to protect the world's tallest and most magnificent trees, the giant sequoias (redwoods) of Mariposa Grove, in the park's southern zone. They are more than 3000 years old, almost 300 ft (92 m) high and measure up to 33 ft (10 m) in diameter.

At the Yosemite Museum visitors can study descriptions and displays of the history and customs of the Miwok and Paiate Indians, present in the area for more than 8000 years.

In 1864 Abraham Lincoln declared Yosemite area "an inalienable public property of the entire nation now and for future generations," and in 1890 the park was established, with an area of over 1200 sq. miles (3107 sq. km). It is noteworthy too that President Lincoln's very important declaration laid the base for the institution, in 1872, of the first national park in the world, Yellowstone.

176 TOP RIGHT A RACCOON TAKES REFUGE INSIDE A TREE TRUNK. IT IS RECOGNIZABLE BY THE DARK MASK AROUND THE EYES.

176-177 THE BRIDALVEIL FALL ARE LIKE A WHITE RIBBON DEFINED AGAINST THE BRIGHT RED OF THE ROCKS.

177 THE YOSEMITE FALLS MAKE AN IMPRESSIVE LEAP OF 2430 FT FT (760 M) AND FLOW INTO ONE OF THE PARK'S MANY WATERCOURSES.

Yosemite

178 TOP THE TRUNK OF THIS SAPLESS TREE, POORLY NOURISHED BY THIN SOIL, HAS BEEN SHAPED BY THE WINDS.

178 BOTTOM THE IMPOSING HALF-DOME OF EL CAPITAN RISES SOLITARY BEYOND THE WOODED VALLEY TRAVERSED BY THE TURBULENT MERCED RIVER.

179 A GROPUP OF YOSEMITE'S HERBIVOROUS MULE DEER GRAZE BENEATH EL CAPITAN, ILLUMINATED BY THE SETTING SUN.

180-181 COVERED BY FOG, ONLY PARTS OF THE IMPOSING CATHEDRAL ROCKS ARE VISIBLE. CATHEDRAL ROCKS IS A MASSIVE ROCKY CREST ON THE SIERRA NEVADA IN THE CENTER OF YOSEMITE PARK.

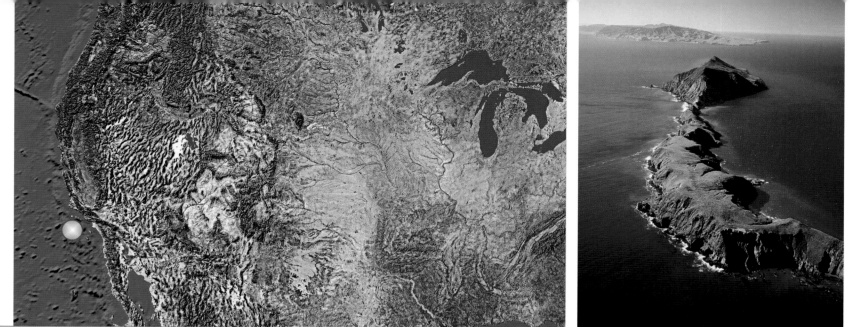

Channel **I**slands **N**ational **P**ark
California

The Channel Islands lie off the coast of California, surrounded by one of the most fish-rich areas of the Pacific Ocean, and are part of a vast national park that in recent years has gained particular popularity as a place to observe the great white shark, the deadly ocean predator who comes to the island waters to hunt sea lions and other large prey. With its 20-foot (6 m) length and about 600 lb (275 kg) weight, its formidable teeth, highly-tuned sensory apparatus and the exceptional speed it is able to reach, the great white shark is one of the major predators of marine mammals in southern Californian waters.

The Channel Islands Park is made up of an archipelago of volcanic islands situated off the coast of Santa Barbara, south of Los Angeles. It was established in 1980 to include Santa Cruz, Santa Rosa, Santa Barbara, Anacapa, and San Miguel (five of the archipelago's eight islands) and an underwater area as well. Overall, the park encompasses almost 250,000 acres (101,200 hectares).

Almost totally devoid of signs of human life, the islands constitute one of the most important reserves for the regional biosphere: there are almost 2000 species of animals and plants present, of which 145 are endemic to the area. Fauna include the island fox, the spotted skunk, and the island night lizard. The islands are also one of the best locations for watching gray whales, dolphins, and other marine mammals during their migratory journey through the Santa Barbara Channel. Other species present are the colossal sea elephants, the eared seal, and the rich fauna of the coastline that is periodically inundated at high tide, providing a food source for migratory seabirds.

The abundance of fish favors a concentration of marine birds that make their nests among the rocks and fish in the sea. This plentiful food supply creates dense flocks of brown pelicans, marvelous divers who plummet vertically into the water like harpoons, as well as seagulls, terns, shearwaters and fulmarine petrels.

In order to protect birdlife, particularly during the nesting season, and other forms of wild life, visits to the Channel Islands are rigidly controlled, even at the day-trip level.

182 TOP RIGHT ANACAPA ISLAND, AT THE END OF THE RAINY SEASON, TAKES OF A SHINY GREEN COLOR DUE TO THE GROWTH, ON ITS SUMMIT, OF FLOURISHING MEADOWS.

182-183 A GLIMPSE OF THE SEA CLIFFS OF ANACAPA ISLAND CAN BE CAUGHT FROM THE COAST. THE OTHER ISLANDS WHICH FORM PART OF THE PROTECTED AREA ARE SANTA CRUZ, SANTA ROSA, SAN MIGUEL AND SANTA BARBARA.

183 DURING SPRING, THE COAST OF CALIFORNIA'S WILDLIFE HAVEN IS COVERED BY A CARPET OF MULTICOLORED FLOWERS.

Channel Islands

184 ROCKS CARVED BY THE SEA TAKE ON FANTASTIC SHAPES LIKE THE GREAT ARCH WHICH RISES DIRECTLY FROM THE CONSTANTLY AGITATED WATERS.

185 TOP GRAY WHALES PASS THROUGH THE PART OF THE SEA INCLUDED IN THE PROTECTED AREA DURING THEIR LONG VOYAGE WHICH WILL TAKE THEM TO THE ARCTIC SEAS.

185 CENTER THE BROWN PELICAN IS A SKILLFUL FISHER WHICH CATCHES ITS PREY BY DIVING FOR FISH FROM THE AIR.

185 BOTTOM SEALS AND SEA LIONS REST IN POINT BENNET BAY IN SAN MIGUEL ISLAND.

186 TOP LEFT A FIELD OF LONG STELES OF ALGAE CHARACTERIZES THE MARINE LANDSCAPE.

186 TOP RIGHT A FISH WITH IMPRESSIVE FINS HIDES AMONGST THE SEAWEEDS.

186-187 THE SOUTHERN COAST OF CALIFORNIA IS VERY RICH IN MARINE FAUNA.

187 TOP A PAINTED GREENLING, WIDESPREAD IN THE PACIFIC COAST, RECOGNIZABLE BY THE COLORED STRIPS ALONG HIS BODY.

187 BOTTOM FIELDS OF ANEMONES COVER ENTIRE PARTS OF THE MARINE DEPTHS.

188-189 ATTRACTED BY THE NUMEROUS SEA LIONS AND SEA ELEPHANTS, THE WHITE SHARK HAUNTS THESE WATERS OFTEN OVER 20 FT (6 M) IN LENGTH, OF HUGE WEIGHT, FORMIDABLE DENTAL STRUCTURE, IMPROVED SENSORY SYSTEM AND ITS EXCEPTIONAL SPEED, THE SHARK IS ONE OF THE MOST EFFICIENT PREDATORS OF THE OCEAN.

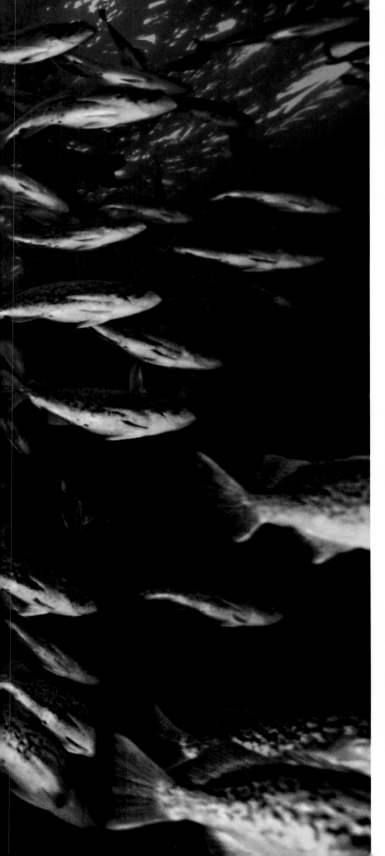

Hawaii Volcanoes National Park
Hawaiian Islands

The Hawaiian archipelago has long felt the effects of human colonization, which has brought, in the span of some two and a half centuries, the disappearance of many plant and animal species and the endangerment of numerous others. A case in point is the nene – the Hawaiian goose – an elegant waterfowl destroyed in its wild state in the 1950s, then saved only because a few specimens raised in captivity were able to reproduce and begin a new lineage. The Monaca seal was also at risk of extinction, and was saved at the last minute by the institution of protected marine reserves and other protected areas. This seal is one of three species of Monaca seal; a second is found in the Mediterranean and the third (though probably now extinct) was native to the Caribbean.

The Hawaii Volcanoes National Park, which includes two active volcanoes, can be called a "vertical development park" since it ranges from beaches bathed by warm tropical waters to the snowcapped peak of Mauna Loa (almost 13,000 ft/3960 m) and the still-smoking caldera of Kilauea. The park is a true laboratory for volcanologists who study the formation of the

archipelago's individual islands – some of the most isolated in the world, situated in the middle of the Pacific, at a distance of approximately 2500 miles (4025 km) from the nearest continent.

The Hawaiian Islands have five active volcanoes, with spectacular eruptions of fountains and streams of lava. The islands are part of a range that was formed over 70 million years ago by the movement of the ocean floor, above a continuing "hot spot" characterized by a strong upthrusts of magmatic material from the Earth's crust.

As a result of the archipelago's isolation, there are numerous species of indigenous plants and animals; in fact, they make up more than 90 percent of those present on the islands. This very high level of biodiversity, even higher that that of the Galapagos, but it is threatened by many dangers, among which are the decline of habitats beyond the park's boundaries, the prevalence of fires, and the invasion of external species brought in by man. Some of the species were purposely introduced into the area by white colonists; for example, the goats, the pig, and the mongoose, while others are the result of "clandestine" immigration, and include rats and numerous harmful insects. In the event, these intruders destroyed the broods and offspring of many of the islands' delicate bird species, which often make their nests on the ground, exposed to predators.

The national park is also of notable anthropological and ethnographic interest because it contains evidence of the ancient Polynesian peoples who reached Hawaii from the Marquesas Islands some 1600 years ago. Anthropologists the world over have come to the Hawaiian Islands to study the long well-preserved but now increasingly threatened social system and characteristics of the population.

Hawaii National Park was established in 1916 and became Hawaii Volcanoes National Park in 1961. It then became an International Biosphere Reserve in 1980 and a World Heritage Site in 1987. It encompasses 333,000 acres (135,000 hectares).

190 VOLCANIC ERUPTIONS ARE
SOMETIMES CHARACTERIZED BY
SUDDEN EXPLOSIONS WHICH HURL
STONES AND ASHES INTO THE AIR.

190-191 AN EXCEPTIONAL VIEW OF AN
ERUPTION OF KILAUEA VOLCANO IN THE
HAWAII ISLANDS' ARCHIPELAGO.

191 TOP LEFT THE LAVA THAT DOES NOT
FLOW OUT OF THE ERUPTING CONE
FILLS UP THE CRATER AND FORMS
SMALL BASINS.

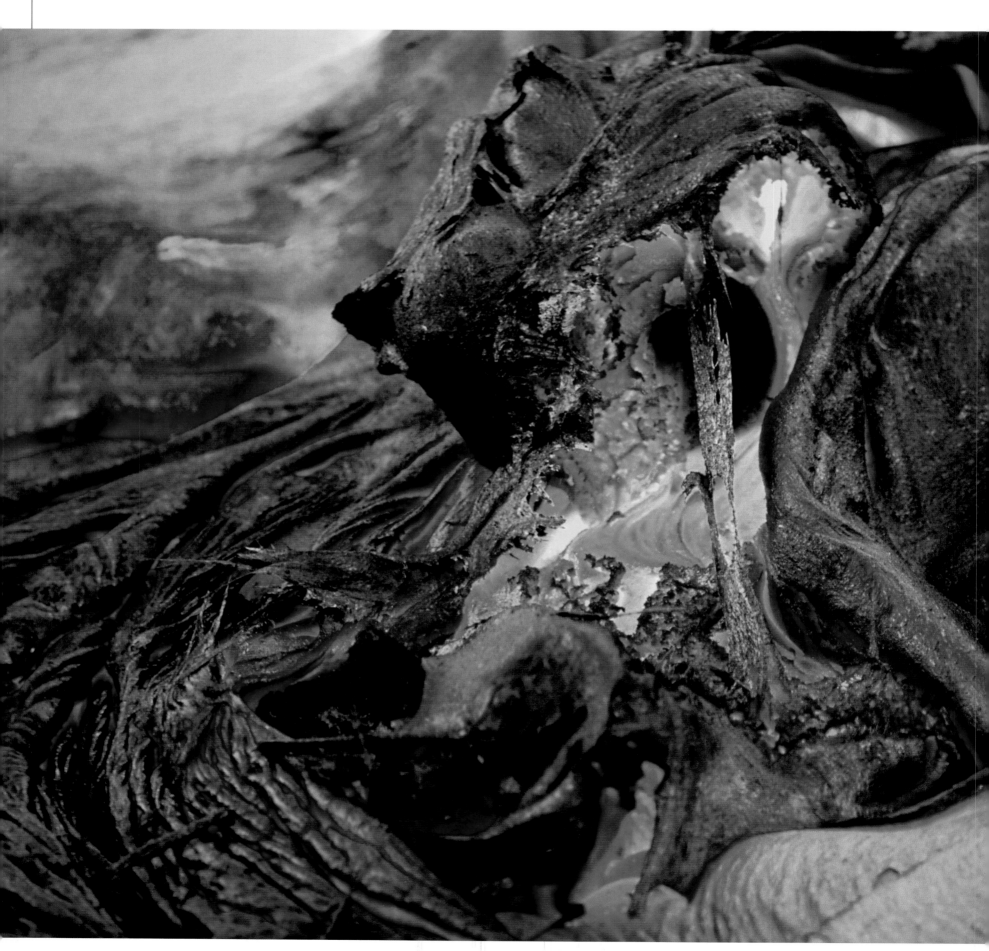

192-193 MAGMA, STILL LIQUID AND EXTREMELY HOT, MAKES ITS WAY BETWEEN COLUMNS OF NOW
COLD AND SOLID LAVA.

193 THE PROCESS AND THE TIMEFRAME OF THE LAVA'S COOLING DETERMINE THE APPEARANCE
OF THE INSULATED LANDSCAPES WHICH, WITH TIME, ARE COVERED BY VEGETATION.

194-195 ERUPTION AFTER ERUPTION, LAVA ACCUMULATES LAYER UPON LAYER TO FORM
A FAIRYTALE-LIKE DESIGN.

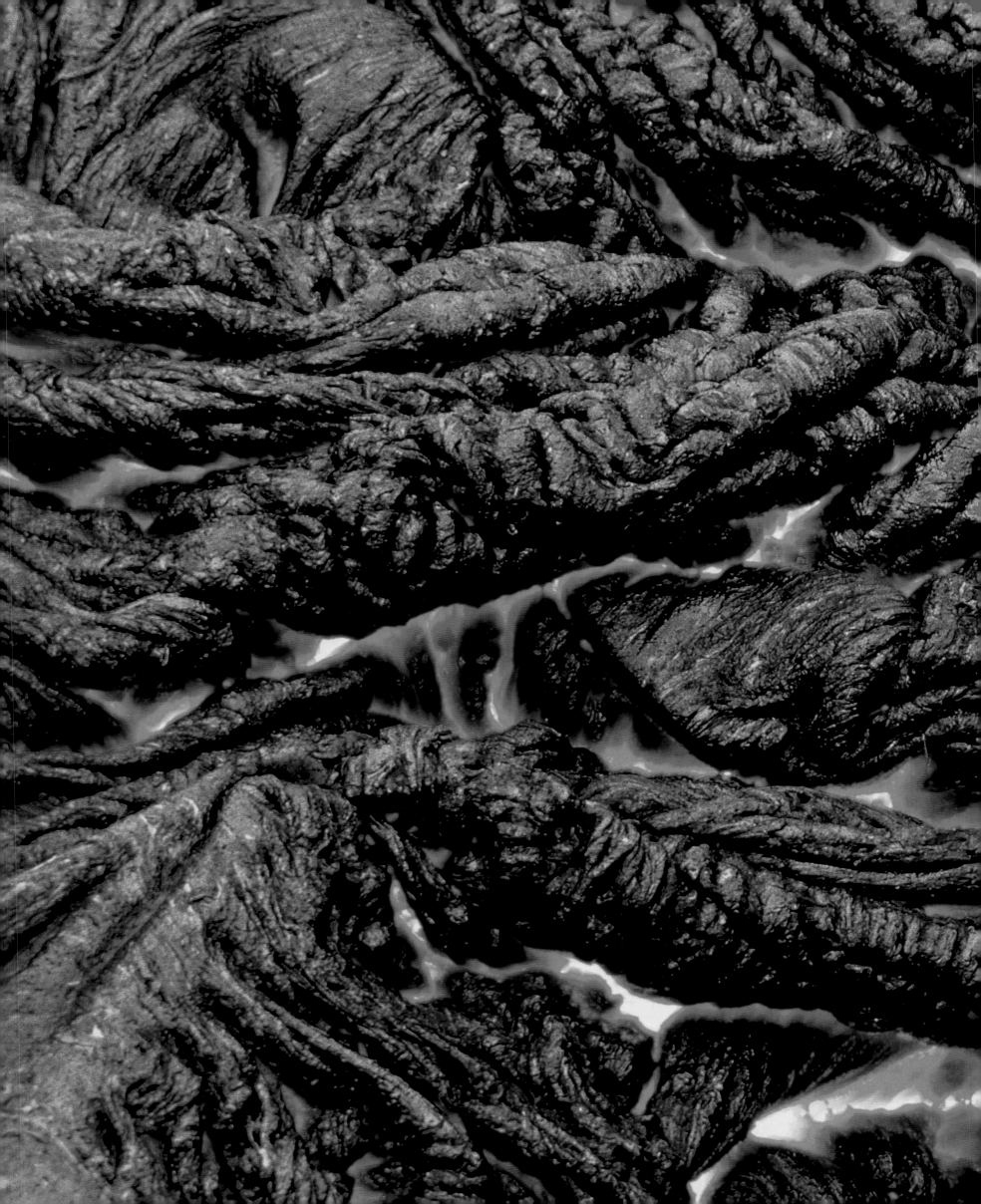

Monument Valley
Utah/Arizona

196 THE LANDSCAPE AT TIMES
EXPANDS, TAKING ON LARGE
PROPORTIONS AND ENDLESS HORIZONS
WHICH ARE LESS OFTEN FOUND IN
OTHER PARTS OF THE NEW WORLD.

196-197 AND 197 TOP LEFT
OVER THE MILLENNIA, WEATHERING
FACTORS SCULPT THE ROCK INTO
IMPRESSIVE ARCHITECTURAL
CONFIGURATIONS.

197 TOP CENTER THE PLANTS' CAPACITY
TO GROW TO SUCH SUBSTANTIAL
PROPORTIONS IN SUCH A BARREN
ENVIRONMENT SEEMS MIRACULOUS.

Though it is neither a National Park nor a Biosphere Reserve but a Navajo Nation Tribal Park encompassing 29,817 acres (12,066 hectares), Monument Valley is one of the most spectacular places on Earth. From a primarily flat landscape, made of often changing sands, rise imposing rocky formations, real towers that have made up the scenery of many Western films and that today can be seen from State Highway 163 that runs from Kayenta in Arizona to Mexican Hat in Utah.

Every peak in Monument Valley has a name, among the most famous of which are Castle Butte, Natani Tso and Brigham's Tomb. Castle Butte is surely one the most photographed rock formations of this vast area that has been shaped and formed by external forces over millions of years. Because of rain, wind and freezing, the rocky bastions of Monument Valley continue to change form from year to year, though imperceptibly.

Extremely hot in summer, and freezing in winter when the snow cloaks the peaks and valleys, Monument Valley is not an easy place for wild plants and animals to live. In many areas, vegetation is quite scarce, represented mostly by grass species that are proof of a miraculous ability to grow in such an inhospitable environment. After the scarce spring rainfall, Monument Valley takes on a more verdant appearance.

Wildlife includes the most adaptable predators of North America, including the coyote and puma that have their dens among the rocks and hunt for rabbits, deer, birds and other medium-sized animals. Birds are well represented, as are reptiles, the animals that are better adapted than others to surviving endless periods of drought.

Most of the area was the land of the Navajo Indian tribe, who learned how to live in such a dry and unwelcoming environment and who left many traces of their existence, a presence radically erased by the advent of white colonization which, however, has not erased the beauty of this land of infinite horizons.

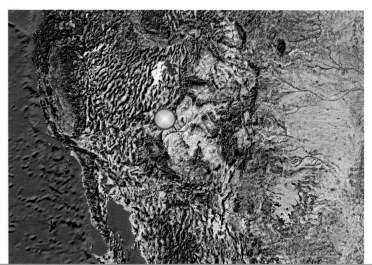

198 TOP FOLLOWING THE SCARCE SPRING RAINFALLS, MONUMENT VALLEY TAKES
ON A GREENER THAN USUAL APPEARANCE.

198 BOTTOM MOST OF THE INHABITANTS OF THE UNITED STATES OF AMERICA
CONSIDER THIS PARK TO BE A SYMBOL OF THE FAR WEST AND OF THE EPIC PIONEERS.

199 THE SHADOWS OF NIGHT STRETCH OUT OVER THE VALLEY, AT THE BOTTOM
OF THE BASTIONS AND ROCK COLUMNS.

200 TOP A MOUNTAIN LION VENTURES IN THE ARID ENVIRONS SEARCHING FOR FOOD.

200 BOTTOM A COYOTE ALMOST SEEMS TO HESITATE AS IT FACES THE SANDY EXPANSE IN SEARCH OF PREY.

200-201 DEAD TREES RAISE THEIR BRANCHES TOWARDS THE SKY. IN THE BACKGROUND, THE ROCK GIANTS
SEEM TO LIFT THEIR GAZE TOWARDS THE HORIZON.

201 TOP LEFT MOUNTAIN LION CUBS GROW UP PROTECTED IN LAIRS FROM HOLLOWS BETWEEN THE ROCKS
WHERE THE SUN'S HEAT IS LESS OPPRESSIVE.

201 TOP RIGHT THE PARK IS, MOST OF ALL, THE HOME OF MANY SPECIES OF REPTILES WHICH ARE WELL
ADAPTED TO PROLONGED DROUGHTS.

202 ALMOST IMPERCEPTIBLY, MONUMENT VALLEY'S ROCKY
BASTIONS CHANGE SHAPE OVER THE YEARS, CARVED BY
WIND, RAIN AND COLD.

202-203 THE ROCK TOWERS' OUTLINE HAS, BY NOW, BECOME
A CLASSIC ELEMENT OF MOST OF THE WESTERNS
MADE IN USA.

204-205 EVERY PEAK OF MONUMENT VALLEY HAS ITS OWN
NAME. FROM THE FOG EMERGES CASTLE BUTTE ON THE LEFT,
AT THE CENTER THERE IS NATANI TSO (BIG LEADER) AND, ON
THE RIGHT, BRIGHAM'S TOMB.

Grand Canyon National Park
Arizona

The Colorado River flows into the Gulf of California after making a long journey through the arid and rocky zones of the southwestern United States. The landscape is familiar to audiences the world over because it is the film setting for so many Westerns. The Grand Canyon in particular, an immense and startlingly deep incision that the river has made in the sedimentary rock over millions of years, is a true star in the history of cinema.

The national park of 1.2 million acres (485,000 hectares) that protects this grandiose geological phenomenon is perhaps America's most famous park, known the world over. It is certainly one of the most frequently visited, well-known and loved.

The Grand Canyon is approximately 280 miles (450 km) long, more than 5250 feet (1600 m) deep, and neighboring ranges rise as high as 9200 feet (2804 m). The Canyon is a geologist's paradise: in it, as in a specialized history book, one can read the story of the Earth over the last 2 billion years. In fact, various geological eras are visible, revealed by erosion and by vertical tectonic movements of the area (from the Proterozoic to today): complete formations and geological layers are ordered one on top of another. Many are very old, beginning with the Vishnu schists that date back to almost 2 billion years ago.

Despite the aridness of the climate, the park is home to a great variety of environments typical of the Rocky Mountain region. They range from sheltering woods along riverbanks, to the evocative forests formed by giant juniper trees, to the caves with typical troglophilic fauna of bats and invertebrates. Because of the variety of natural environments it includes, the park offers visitors the chance to take a trip through the main ecosystems of North America, as if traveling from Canada to Mexico, from woodlands to desert. In fact, five of the seven "life zones" of the United States are present, as are three of the four desert types. There are also numerous protected indigenous species at hand: more than 1500 plants, 355 birds, 89 mammals, 47 reptiles, 17 fish and 9 amphibians.

Not to be missed are the coyotes, mule deer, bobcats, mountain lions and the Kaibab squirrel, or the cacti and blackbrush. Among the most attention-grabbing avian species are the golden eagle, the peregrine falcon, and the red-tailed buzzard.

The Grand Canyon was declared a National Monument in 1908, a National Park in 1919 and a World Heritage Site in 1979, this last designation recognizing the existence of almost 500 archaeological sites.

206 ROCKS ERODED BY THE WATERS OF THE COLORADO RIVER FORM DEEP GORGES WHERE IT IS POSSIBLE TO READ THE GEOLOGICAL HISTORY OF NORTH AMERICA.

206-207 VARIOUS CLIMATIC ZONES EXIST IN THE AREA: SNOW IS PRESENT AT HIGH ALTITUDES THROUGHOUT THE WINTER.

207 TOP LEFT THE CANYON HAS A DEPTH OF 5250 FT (1600 M) IN SOME AREAS; ITS WIDTH CAN BE MEASURED IN MILES.

ANYON NATIONAL PARK - ARIZONA - GRAND CANYON NA

208 TOP WATER ACCUMULATES IN THE LOWEST PART OF THE CANYON, MAKING IT POSSIBLE FOR VARIOUS ARBOREAL SPECIES TO SURVIVE.

208-209 AND 209 WATER'S EROSIVE ACTION HAS REVEALED THE CANYON WALLS' ROCK STRATA. AT LEAST 12 STRATA, WITH DIFFERENT PHYSICAL AND MORPHOLOGICAL CHARACTERISTICS, HAVE BEEN IDENTIFIED. SOME STRATA CONTAIN FOSSIL EVIDENCE OF A VARIETY OF PREVIOUS FAUNA AND FLORA.

210-211 MANY PROTECTED SPECIES INHABIT THE PARK, INCLUDING THE MOUNTAIN LION, A FELINE WITH A VERY VARIED DIET AND WHICH LEADS A SOLITARY LIFE, ADAPTING ITSELF WITH EASE TO THE CLIMATIC DIVERSITIES EXISTING IN THE PARK.

Grand Canyon

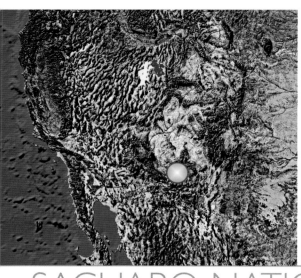

212 TOP RIGHT THIS HARRIS HAWK HAS FOUND REFUGE IN THE THORNY FOLIAGE OF A SAGUARO.

212-213 THE NATIONAL PARK'S BARREN LANDSCAPE HIDES A FERTILE LIFE.

213 THE SAGUARO CAN SURVIVE FOR CENTURIES; IT REPRODUCES ITSELF ONLY UNDER VERY FAVORABLE CONDITIONS.

214-215 CACTI STEMS WATER IN PERIODS OF DROUGHT, WHEREAS THE LEAVES HAVE BEEN REDUCED TO THORNS SO AS TO AVOID LOSS OF LIQUIDS.

Saguaro National Park
Arizona

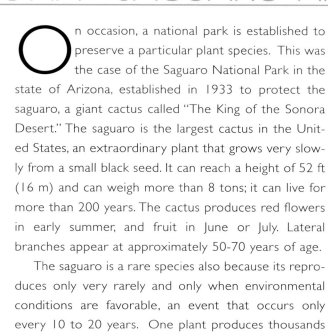

On occasion, a national park is established to preserve a particular plant species. This was the case of the Saguaro National Park in the state of Arizona, established in 1933 to protect the saguaro, a giant cactus called "The King of the Sonora Desert." The saguaro is the largest cactus in the United States, an extraordinary plant that grows very slowly from a small black seed. It can reach a height of 52 ft (16 m) and can weigh more than 8 tons; it can live for more than 200 years. The cactus produces red flowers in early summer, and fruit in June or July. Lateral branches appear at approximately 50-70 years of age.

The saguaro is a rare species also because its reproduces only very rarely and only when environmental conditions are favorable, an event that occurs only every 10 to 20 years. One plant produces thousands of seeds per year, but very few are able to survive and grow in such a difficult environment. The desert receives less than 8 in. (2.5 cm) of rainfall per year, and this plant has adapted in many ways that allow it to conserve water: with its prickles, its external waxy layer, its spongy internal ribs and its roots, penetrating only about 3 to 4 in. (7.5 to 10 cm) into the ground, spread out in a radius equal to the height of the plant.

For thousands of years the inhabitants of the desert, the Tohono O'Odham Indians, harvested its fruits, similar to large figs, using long rods to knock them down, analogous to shaking nut trees. They made the fruits into preserves, syrups, and a type of wine used for religious ceremonies. The harvest of the fruits of the saguaro marked the beginning of the new year. The seeds of this plant were also utilized, as were the woody interiors, which were used for constructing shelters and fences.

The protection of the saguaro has also brought the protection of all other species of the ecological community of the Sonora Desert, which surpasses all other deserts on Earth for it variety of living forms of flora and fauna. Nonetheless, the saguaro, in whose trunk small owls and woodpeckers nest, remains a very vulnerable plant: animals eat its seeds and sprouts, and the biggest ones can be knocked down by lightning and wind. It is to be hoped that the park area of 91,000 acres (37,000 hectares) will provide a safe haven for the saguaro and other endangered cacti.

Cape Cod National Seashore
Massachussets

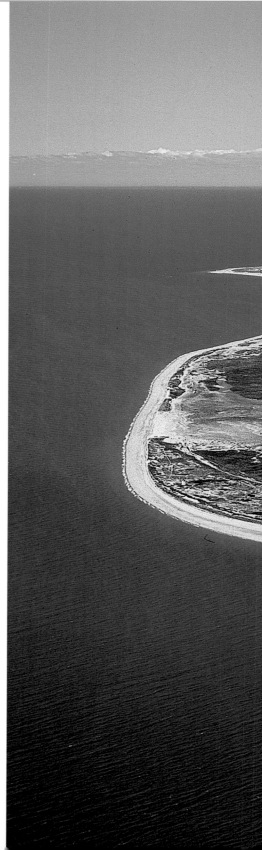

The tide is the leading force of the protected area of Cape Cod, marking time with its ebbing and flowing. The marine fauna takes the upper hand when the water rises, submerging vast stretches of coastline, then gives way to land organisms that come to feast on the food made available by the ocean waters once they have receded.

Seen from above, the Cape Cod peninsula has a unique and thus unmistakable hook shape. Formed by moraine deposits left by glaciers more than 3000 years ago, the Cape is a long stretch of coastline that extends more than 60 miles (100 km) into the Atlantic Ocean, with a shoreline that dries out or is submerged depending upon the tide. The Cape is continuously shaped and reshaped by strong ocean currents; these, in surging round Monomoy Island, create and destroy shallows, sandbars and beaches.

In all, the Cape is a mutable landscape, difficult to depict on a geographic map as powerful erosive phenomena and the forces of nature continuously construct and reconstruct the coastline.

The peninsula has more than 30 freshwater ponds that together with the swamps and temporary brackish pools are resting and feeding grounds for many migratory birds. The area is particularly important for avian life in that it contains populations of more than 30 percent of the bird species listed as rare and endangered in Massachussetts as a whole.

For the most part deforested by European colonists between the 18th and 20th centuries, the Cape is still home to a few pine and oak forests subject to continual summer fires but also responsible for the creation of unique land habitats, some open and wooded, others limited to peat and heather.

In terms of human history, in 1620, Cape Cod was the first shoreline seen from the *Mayflower*, which carried a group of Pilgrims aboard who belonged to the Puritans, a sect persecuted by the established Church of England. The Pilgrims' first contact with the New World at Cape Cod was then followed by the first act of self-government on North American soil: the election of a member of their community to the office of governor.

216 AND 216-217 CAPE COD, WHICH EXTENDS OVER 60 MILES (97 KM) INTO THE ATLANTIC OCEAN, HAS A CURIOUS HOOK-LIKE FORM. IT IS MADE UP OF MORAINE DEPOSITS LEFT BY GLACIERS MORE THAN 3000 YEARS AGO.

217 TOP LEFT BETWEEN THE 17TH AND 20TH CENTURIES, EUROPEAN SETTLERS LARGELY DEFORESTED CAPE COD. THEY PLANTED (AND LATER ABANDONED) CEREALS AND VINES, WHICH LED TO THE DEVELOPMENT OF MOORLAND AND LATER THE GROWTH OF WOODLANDS.

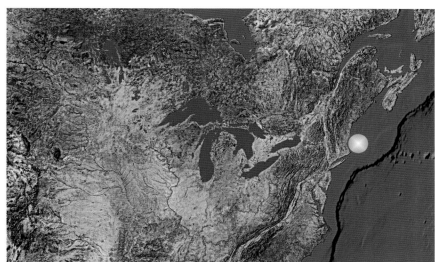

218 TOP THE PROTECTED AREA IS HOME TO ABOUT THIRTY FRESHWATER PONDS, SUPPLIED BY THE WATER TABLE AND BY RAIN. AN EXCEPTIONAL VARIETY OF AQUATIC BIRDS VISIT THE PONDS.

218 BOTTOM THE IMPORTANCE OF THE MARINE FAUNA CHARACTERIZES THIS PARK. IT IS POSSIBLE TO CATCH SIGHT OF WHALES ON THEIR WAY TOWARDS THE ARCTIC.

218-219 A GREAT BLUE HERON HAS CAUGHT HIS PREY, HARPOONING IT WITH HIS LONG AND SHARP BEAK. MANY SPECIES OF AQUATIC BIRDS REST IN THE HUMID AREA DURING THEIR MIGRATIONS.

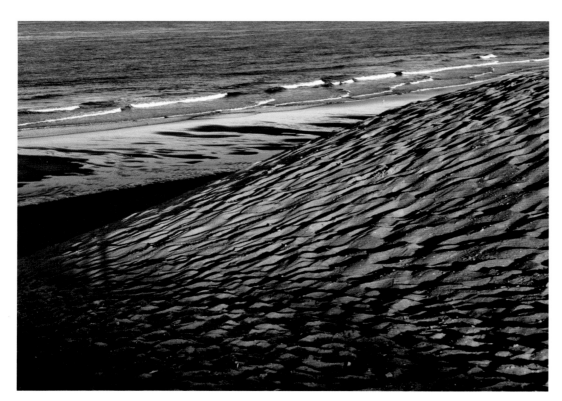

Cape Cod

Chesapeake and Ohio Canal National Historic Park

Maryland

The historical value of this park and its canal is exceptional, as demonstrated by the more than 1300 structures built over the course of centuries to control the water: dikes, pumps, aqueducts, locks, and artificial canals – all constructed to make the waterways the favored way to travel in the area.

This park, which borders the Potomac River from Cumberland, Maryland to Washington, D.C., is also rich in biodiversity and hosts more than 1200 plant species; of them, 150 are classified as rare, endangered, or in danger of extinction: the highest concentration of at-risk flora in all of the Eastern United States. Along the Potomac, in addition, species of northern origin meet with others of southern origin and small nuclei of plants of western origin grow in the fields.

The canal begins just under the impressive Potomac Falls and proceeds westward, crossing areas that are geomorphologically diverse: Piedmont, the Blue Ridge Mountains and the Ridge Valley. Over millions of years the Potomac has modified the shape of the valley where the Chesapeake and Ohio Canal is located, and the rocks today exposed by erosion recall the process of the formation of the North American continental mass following the collision with other plates, which now lie beneath the ocean. Men have always been attracted to this land: the Indian populations used the river as a means of reaching the Appalachian Mountains. They also managed to build dams to form small ponds for fishing. Canals too played a role in the colonization of the West; they were built to make navigation easier, bypassing rapids and rocky ravines.

The Chesapeake and Ohio Canal was for a long time the principal means of communication within a significant and developing area, and only with the expansion of the railroad was a project for a waterway that connected east and west abandoned. Yet, even today, many communities depend on the Potomac for their drinking water and energy.

Worth noting is the presence of the Potomac gorges, some of the most striking and important wild lands of the eastern United States and their numerous old gold mines, whose operation dates back to historic times, with many of their structures still partially intact.

220 A FOREST OF DECIDUOUS TREES DISPLAYS ITS BRIGHTER COLORS AT THE START OF AUTUMN.

220-221 THE PARK HAS MANY WATERCOURSES WHICH MEANDER THROUGH WOODS AND GRASSLANDS TO REACH CHESAPEAKE BAY, IN CALVERT COUNTY, MARYLAND.

221 TOP RIGHT THE HENS IN THIS COLONY OF TERNS HAVE LAID THEIR EGGS ON A SHORE OF CHESAPEAKE BAY.

222-223 AN ARC OF THE POTOMAC RIVER EMBRACES A BROAD SPREAD OF DECIDUOUS TREES: MAPLES, OAKS AND OTHER SPECIES GRADUALLY TAKE ON FALL'S WARM COLORS.

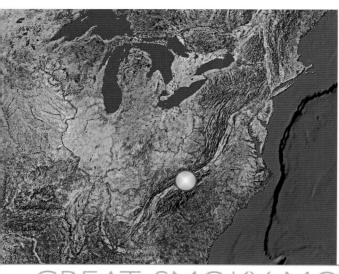

224 TOP RIGHT AND 225 BOTTOM
THE PARK'S FORESTS, LIKE THIS ONE
IN CADES COVE, ARE PREDOMINANTLY
MADE UP OF DECIDUOUS TREES.

224-225 THE FOG TAKES SOME TIME TO
FADE FROM MORTON OVERLOOK'S
VALLEYS.

225 TOP A GROUP OF WHITE-TAILED
DEER, LED BY A MALE, RUN AWAY.

226-227 FALL OFFERS STUNNING
SIGHTS: AT TIMES THE FOG SEEMS
TO BE ENTANGLED AMONG
THE TREES.

Great Smoky Mountains National Park
North Carolina

The southern spur of the Appalachian mountain range marks the border between Tennessee and North Carolina. In the middle of this range is the Great Smoky Mountains National Park, world-famous for the beauty of its landscapes and for the countless forms of animal and plant life that coexist with the vestiges of the original Appalachian mountain culture.

The Appalachians are among the oldest mountain ranges in the world, an orogenic belt that formed in the Devonian period from the collision of the American and European plates. The glaciers of the last Ice Age spared this region, which then became the refuge for many animal and plant species coming from neighboring areas, a series of migrations that partially explain the park's great biodiversity. The Great Smoky Mountains – also called The Smokies – are the highest range in the Apppalachian chain; some peaks in the park area reach heights of 6600 ft (2010 m). The peaks include Mount Le Conte Towers and Clingmans Dome. The climate varies widely from zone to zone and presents considerable seasonal variations; rainfall, very abundant in the higher ground, feeds 1900 miles (3050 km) of a water system composed of rivers, streams, creeks and waterfalls.

At least five different types of forest can be identified In the park, some types dominated by conifers, others by deciduous trees. A quarter of these forests are classified as temperate primigenial forest, that is, completely devoid of any signs of human intervention: in total these sections amount to one of the biggest blocks of residual temperate forest still present in North America. Botanists have inventoried at least 5000 species of plant, of which many are rare, endangered or indigenous

The park's wildlife is just as abundant, with more than 10,000 wildlife species officially catalogued, but some estimates taken from census samples suggest that a much larger number of species are living in the protected area. Mammals including muskrats, the red fox, and the southern flying squirrel are all well represented, and white-tailed deer and wild hogs can be seen.

The park can claim a very successful history of species reintroduction, a process designed to bring back an animal or plant species to an area where it had become extinct because of human interventions. Many animals have been brought back to the Appalachians to complete the mosaic of wild life that includes native species of great importance such as the black bear, whose current population is estimated to be 1800. Salamanders are constitute a highlight for the park – which in fact claims the title of "World Capital of the Salamander" because more than 30 species have been identified there. These extremely interesting long-tailed and normally secretive amphibians have a particular biological cycle which, during their reproductive period, drives them to enter the water and make themselves visible. The park was established in 1934, declared an International Biosphere Reserve in 1976, and a World Heritage Site in 1983.

228-229 A LARGE PART OF LITTLE PIGEON RIVER'S INITIAL COURSE IS IN FACT
A TORRENT WITH TURBULENT AND CAPRICIOUS WATERS.

229 TOP THIS BOBCAT, SAFE IN THE BRANCHES OF A BIRCH, IS PREPARING AN ATTACK.

229 BOTTOM MORTON OVERLOOK OFFERS A MAGNIFICENT VIEW
OF THE SUGAR LAND VALLEY, HERE SEEN DURING ONE OF THE FIRST
WINTER SNOWFALLS.

Everglades National Park
Florida

Trees that grow right in the water, creating intricate and almost impenetrable forests, wide ponds bursting with life, flown over by flocks of herons and multicolored spoonbills, and dense coastal forests and swampy beaches where freshwater meets seawater in a rich cocktail of life forms, constitute the heart of the Everglades, the most extensive wilderness area in the subtropical zone of the United States. The Everglades were called Pa-hay-okee (Grassy Water) by the Calusa Indians because their principal characteristic is the wide expanses of grassland temporarily flooded by rains and the overflow of the waterways. Along the shoreline the mangroves form a dense plant barrier that withstands the salt water because of its particular adaptations.

The Everglades provide an environment well-suited to the wading birds of many species: white and tricolor herons, egrets, pink spoonbills, and ibis live in great numbers in these shallow waters that offer mollusks, insects, crustaceans, and small fish for every type of hunting and every type of beak. Hidden in the water, the alligator waits for its prey: a deer, a bird, a raccoon, or any other animal that happens within reach of its jaws.

The alligator can grow to 13 ft (4 m) in length and 600 lbs (272 kg). Females deposit their eggs in nests hidden in mounds of dirt and vegetation and guard them devotedly until hatched.

This too is the kingdom of the protected Florida manatee, a rare aquatic mammal that feeds on plants that grow on the waterbed. There are many other endangered species in the park, such as the Florida puma and some ocean turtles.

Before it was partially drained at the beginning of the 1900s, the wetlands of the Everglades were an area about 125 miles (200 km) long and about 62 miles (100 km), which extended from the Bay of Florida to Lake Okeechobee, where most of the water originated.

In 1920 an extensive system of dikes and canals was built around the lake in an attempt to hold back the water that often inundated the surrounding areas, whipped up and driven by the frequent hurricanes that strike the area.

Today the drawing-off of water for agricultural irrigation projects, the resulting fall in the water level, and pollution due to fast-growing urban and industrial areas, constitute serious threats that the park must face.

The Everglades Park, with recent additions, now encompasses approximately 1.5 million acres (600,000 hectares).

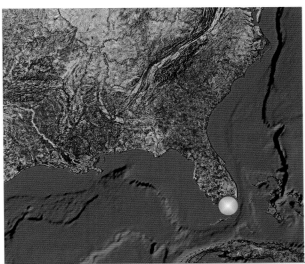

230 TOP THE FLORIDA MOUNTAIN LION
HAS A DARKER COAT THAN ITS
COUNTERPARTS WHICH LIVE IN THE
WESTERN REGIONS OF AMERICA.

230 BOTTOM, 230-231 AND 231 TOP
RIGHT THE LANDSCAPE IS A MOSAIC OF
FORESTS AND PONDS, WITH AQUATIC
BIRDS FLYING ABOVE IT. A BELT OF
MANGROVES GROWS ALONG THE
SHORELINE; IT IS AN IMPORTANT
ECOSYSTEM AND PROVIDES A
NURSERY FOR MARINE FAUNA.

232 TOP A HERON MOTIONLESS IN THE VEGETATION WAITS TO CATCH ITS PREY. THESE BIRDS PREFERS HUMID COAST ZONES, BUT THEIR LONG NECKS ENABLE THEM ALSO TO FISH IN DEEP WATER.

232 BOTTOM WETLANDS, MORASSES, MANGROVE FORESTS AND WOODS ARE THE IDEAL REFUGE FOR VARIOUS SPECIES OF BIRDS.

232-233 FLORIDA IS THE REALM OF THE ALLIGATOR, ONE OF THE LARGEST REPRESENTATIVES OF THE CROCODILIA ORDER, WHICH HAD 23 SPECIES IN VARIOUS REGION OF THE WORLD.

233 TOP LEFT THE LARGE MANGROVE FOREST IS ONE OF THE CHARACTERISTICS OF THE PARK. THIS TYPE OF FLORA DEVELOPS IN ALONG SHORELINES, AND FLOURISHES IN A SALT-WATER ENVIRONMENT.

233 TOP RIGHT TURTLES ARE ANOTHER REPTILE SPECIES WHICH LIVE IN THIS TROPICAL WETLAND REGION.

234 TOP   IN THE HEART OF THE EVERGLADES, WHERE FRESHWATER MEETS SEAWATERTHE EVERGLADES, WHERE FRESHWATER MEETS SEAWATER CONDITIONS PROMOTE A RICH MIX OF SPECIES.

234 CENTER AND 234-235   SWAMPS AND PONDS ABOUND IN THIS PARK. THESE FEATURES HAVE GIVEN THE PARK THE NAME "RIVER OF GRASS."

234 BOTTOM   MANGROVES GROW IN COASTAL ZONES. THEY SURVIVE SALT WATER THANKS TO SPECIFIC COPING ADAPTATIONS.

235 TOP   A RIVER FOLLOWS A MEANDERING COURSE AS IT FLOWS THROUGH A DENSE FOREST.

Alto Golfo de California y Delta del Rio Colorado Reserve Biosphere

Sonora

The Sea of Cortez extends north, like a long tongue between the mountainous and narrow peninsula of Baja California and the western coast of Mexico, becoming narrow itself in the north, in the Alto Golfo de California, before ending at the mouth of the Colorado River. The vegetation of the area above water is rather scarce and scrubby as a result of the very arid climate conditions, which also experience an acutely variable temperature range, both daily and seasonally. In this region, there is a marked contrast between the red, yellow and brown hues of the rocks that are barely or not at all covered by vegetation, and the cobalt blue of the sea that winds in thousands of fjords and coves, creating one of the planet's most complex and productive marine ecosystems. The abundance of nutrients that benefit from active tides helps to promote the development of a rich food chain that leads up to some super predators of great biological interest: among the mammals primarily the odontocete ("toothed") whales and the small dolphin. This latter species assumes particular importance, as does the *Phocoena sinus* porpoise, locally called *vaquita*. It is a species endemic to the Alto Golfo area, classified as "threatened by extinction"; in the early 1990s fewer than 500 of them existed. Among the bird species the osprey, the frigate and the brown pelican are of primary interest. In order to protect the marine mammal and bird species, the Alto Golfo de California y Delta del Rio Colorado Reserve Biosphere was established, encompassing in all 2.3 million acres (930,500) from the northern part of the Sea of Cortez (Alto Golfo), extending south. It was established in 1995 and during a subsequent meeting of the signatories of the Convention on Wetlands of International Importance (the Ramsar Convention) was proposed as a site to be given protected status. It is important not only for the *vaquita*, but because it also safeguards the reproductive sites of many species of birds and fish, such as the totoaba (*Totoaba macdonaldi*), threatened by extinction. The reserve is the first marine area that Mexico formally and strictly protects – and is already attracting an annually increasing number visitors, eager to benefit from the opportunity to observe some of the most interesting inhabitants of the sea in a relatively small area. Though apparently lacking in life forms, the desert environment offers the strange beauty of elegant cacti of varied shapes, some of which explode into brilliant flower after the rains. The plants appear to be regularly spaced between rocks and bare stretches, almost as if a hard-working gardener wanted to lay out a botanical garden to emphasize the strength, and at the same time the fragility, of life in the desert.

236 SEEN FROM ABOVE: THE MARKINGS LEFT BY WATER FROM THE COLORADO RIVER WHICH WAS ABSORBED BY SAND BEFORE IT REACHED THE SEA. THEY ALMOST APPEAR TO BE DRAWINGS.

236-237 THE SO CALLED "COLORED" RIVER FLOWS INTO THE SEA OF CORTEZ, FORMING A WIDE DELTA.

237 TOP LEFT THE UPPER PART OF THE GULF OF CALIFORNIA IS FORMED FROM A DESERT REGION OF ROCKY PEAKS AND NARROW VALLEYS.

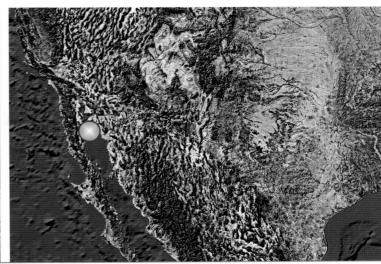

Golfo de California y Delta del Rio Colorado

238 LEFT THE COYOTE MANAGES TO SURVIVE EVEN IN THE HARSHEST OF ENVIRONMENTS, OFTEN NOT FAR AWAY FROM HUMANS.

238 TOP RIGHT BOTH SANDY DUNES AND ROCKY PEAKS ARE FOUND IN THE ALTAR DESERT WITH ITS SCARCE VEGETATION.

238 CENTER RIGHT THE TURKEY VULTURE IS A SCAVENGER BIRD WHICH FEEDS ON THE CARCASSES AND WASTE OF OTHER ANIMALS.

238 BOTTOM RIGHT FOR A FEW WEEKS IN THE YEAR – SOMETIMES IN ALTERNATE YEARS – THE DESERT BRILLIANT WITH FLOWERS, THROUGH WHICH CACTI RISE UP IS .

239 AFTER RAIN SHOWERS THE DESERT IS FILLED WITH MULTI-COLORED FLOWERS AMONG WHICH THE PRIMROSE STANDS OUT.

240 LEFT A PART OF BAJA CALIFORNIA'S NORTHERN COAST, CHARACTERIZED BY A LARGE DESERT ZONE.

240-241 THE SEA OF CORTEZ DIVIDES THE BAJA CALIFORNIA PENINSULA FROM THE MEXICAN COAST.

241 TOP LEFT THE BROWN PELICAN IS A SKILLFUL FISHER AND CAPTURES ITS PREY BY DIVING, SOMETIMES 10 FT (3 M) DEEP.

241 TOP RIGHT THE GULF OF CALIFORNIA IS EXTREMELY RICH IN WHALES, INCLUDING THE GIGANTIC BLUE WHALE.

Complejo Lagunar Ojo de Liebre Biosphere Reserve
Baja California

Like a long bony finger, the peninsula of Baja California extends south from California into the Pacific Ocean, protecting a warm inner body of water, the Sea of Cortez. The Pacific Ocean's waves bathe the peninsula's outer shores; they are often shrouded in morning fogs that break up only toward noon. This stretch of the Pacific coast is a haven for the endangered gray whale, which returns every year to give birth in the calm, fish-filled coastal waters above Vizcaino Bay, a huge crescent-shaped bay protected by the small northward-thrusting peninsula on which the Sierra Vizcaino rises. The bay, close to the coastal range of San Andreas and the Sierra de Santa Clara, is at the midpoint of Baja California, where it divides into northern and southern halves. From a geological standpoint, the Baja California Peninsula represents the continuation of the San Andreas Range and the fault of the same name, and is largely composed of metamorphic and volcanic rock. The peninsula's landscape is quite varied; it includes long beaches of very fine sand, high dunes that look like modest hills, covered with local pioneer plants; areas of desolate rocky territory, rolling inland expanses; and also vast salt deposits. In 1993 the peninsula was designated a World Heritage Site because of it 300 or more archaeological sites and for its cave paintings. These latter date back some 10,000 years and are the creation of an early indigenous population.

The climate is arid, with wide temperature ranges in the central part of the peninsula; it very hot along the coast of the Sea of Cortez but cooler and more humid along Pacific coast. Drought is perhaps the peninsula's most notable characteristic; it has an annual rainfall of only 3 inches (7.6 cm) and with periods of no rain that can last more than three years. During these periods the only steady source of humidity for the desert ecosystem comes from the interaction of the California cold current with warm subtropical water, which produces fog and dew at sunrise. During the cyclone season, from September to December, some rain may fall, and this makes it possible for annual plants to complete a short reproductive cycle. The peninsula, because of the prohibitive conditions of the desert and semi-desert habitats, has remained isolated and is little colonized by humankind. Even today there are many areas in which the level of any human intervention is very low, allowing plant and animal species to continue to prosper. The Baja California Biosphere Reserve is a very important area for nesting and winter shelter for millions of migratory birds (especially ducks and geese) and for the nesting of others such as the golden eagle, the peregrine falcon, the osprey, the crested caracara, and the den owl. Racing though the cacti is the roadrunner cuckoo, and various species of hummingbird dart around, looking for flowers – that vital source of nectar. The Sea of Cortez is home to 38 species of marine mammals, and in the water and along the protected coastline the otter and sea lion thrive. Overall, the Biosphere encompasses over 9650 sq. miles (25,000 sq. km).

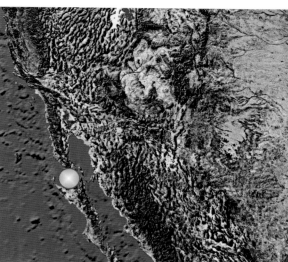

Ojo de Liebre

244 DURING SOME PERIODS OF THE YEAR, THE DUNES WHICH FLANK THE
GUERRERO NEGRO LAGOON'S CALM AND SHALLOW WATERS ARE THE IDEAL PLACE TO
OBSERVE GRAY WHALES.

245 TOP THE DOLPHIN SWIMS IN PACKS OF HUNDREDS IN THE WATERS OF THE BAJA
CALIFORNIA COAST.

245 BOTTOM A HUMPBACK WHALE LEAPING OUT OF THE WATER. THIS CETACEAN
CAN REACH 60 FEET (18 M) IN LENGTH.

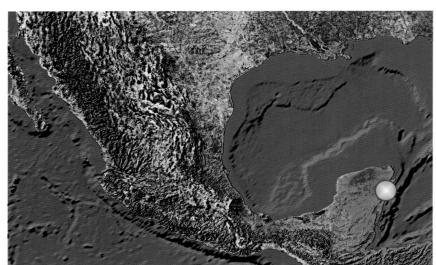

Sian Ka'an Biosphere Reserve
Quintana Roo

On Mexico's Yucatán coast, a short distance from Cancun and Tulum, lies the Biosphere Reserve of Sian Ka'an, a Mayan expression that means "where the sky is born." The humid subtropical climate and the particular morphology of the terrain favor the presence of very diversified habitats that includes forests, grasslands, swamps, cane thickets, and slow rivers as well as the development of plants typical of marshlands and brackish areas. The reserve includes quite a few miles of magnificent Caribbean beaches with an intact coral reef 100 ft (30 m) off the coast. Overall, the reserve hosts an exceptional variety of life forms.

Today the protected area that in the south becomes the wilderness area of Bahia de Espiritu Santo covers 345 sq. miles (890 sq. km) and hosts 318 species of butterflies, 345 species of birds (including parrots, kingfishers, herons, spoonbills and the large jabiru stork), and dozens of species of amphibians, reptiles and mammals.

There are numerous of species of fish thriving in the coral reef (one of the best preserved in the world), as well as in the huge mangrove forest that extends over the area where freshwater meets saltwater. Many endangered species, such as the Caribbean manatee and sea turtles of various kinds (including the loggerhead, flatback and hawksbill) come to lay their eggs between June and August. Among the residents of the reserve, the jaguar – the great feline predator of the neotropical region – deserves special mention. Recent estimates indicate that the reserve's jaguar population of the reserve can be considered one of the best established in Central America because of the abundance of prey such as the peccary, tapir and deer.

Despite that it is relatively young from a geological standpoint – having risen from the sea less than two million years ago – the area is covered by thick vegetation that has had time to diversify into many forms. Plant species amount to more than 1200, of which at least 230 are trees; the percentage of indigenous species is high, approximately 15 percent of the total.

246 TOP RIGHT AND 246-247 A MAZE OF SEA LOCHS AND ISLETS, COVERED BY A DENSE VEGETATION OF MANGROVES, FORMS THE COASTAL PART OF THE PARK.

247 THE JAGUAR IS BECOMING PROGRESSIVELY RARER, AND TODAY THIS FELINE IS CONSIDERED IN DANGER OF EXTINCTION.

248-249 THE POINT OF CONTACT BETWEEN THE LAND ECOSYSTEMS, FRESHWATER ENVIRONMENTS AND THE SEA IS A TERRITORY RICH WITH BIODIVERSITY.

251 TOP THE MANATEE, ALSO KNOWN
AS THE SEA COW, SWIMS IN LOW
DEPTHS, TAKING ITS NOURISHMENT
FROM GRASS AND OTHER
MARINE FLORA.

251 BOTTOM THE SEA TURTLE IS
AMONGST THE RAREST AND MOST
THREATENED OF SPECIES, DUE TO ITS
VALUABLE SHELL. THE SALE AND
PURCHASE OF SEA TURTLES IS
NOW PROHIBITED.

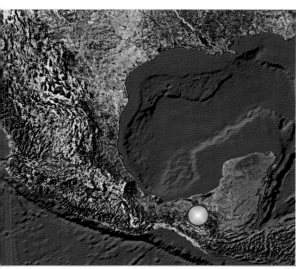

252 TOP RIGHT THERE IS A DISTINCT CONTRAST BETWEEN THE WILD AND PURE ENVIRONMENT OF THE CANYON AND THE LARGELY DEFORESTED AND CULTIVATED ENVIRONMENT OF THE CONFINING HEIGHTS.

252-253 THE ROCKY WALLS WHICH FLANK THE COURSE OF THE GRIJALVA RIVER PRESENT A RICH AND FASCINATING FAUNA AND FLORA.

253 ABOUT 12 MILLION YEARS AGO, THE RIO GRIJALVA CARVED OUT THE SUMIDERO CANYON.

Sumidero Canyon
Chiapas

The harsh and sometimes ominous landscape of the Sumidero region of Chiapas is the result of the work of the water that for millions of years has cut deeply into the rock, carving out ravines and gorges of great depth called barrancos. This result is the work of erosion during rainy periods that alternated with long periods of drought.

When rainfall is more abundant, there is a significant acceleration of violent, wild and unrestrained erosion. The effects of this phenomenon are amplified by the structure of the reliefs and of the water basin that, without real access to the sea because of the coastal mountain ranges of the Pacific and the Sierra Madre, forces the few internal rivers to dig out passageways with barrancos of exceptional proportions.

The Sumidero Canyon is hardly an accessible world; it has been explored only in recent years by experienced naturalists using of the latest tools and techniques in mountain studies and speleology. These aids have allowed them to discover and record the particular biological richness of the microcosms formed by discrete environmental units within the protected area. In fact, in different sections, because of their isolation, unique communities of plants and animals live and prosper, different from those that populate areas that are almost adjoining.

Large numbers of bats, reptiles, amphibians and small ground mammals populate the walls and bottom of the rocky canyons where water flows in torrents after rain but disappears almost completely during long periods of drought. Bird life is of particular note; it includes vultures and many species of birds of prey, as well as miniscule shiny-plumed hummingbirds.

The protected area of 54,470 acres (22,050 hectares) is located in the southern part of Mexico, in the State of Chiapas not far from the city of Tuxtla Gutierrez (which means "The Place of Rabbits").

Sumidero Canyon

254-255 HUMIDITY AND THE SCARCITY OF LIGHT AT THE BOTTOM OF THE CANYON ALLOW FOR THE DEVELOPMENT OF PARTICULAR FORMS OF FERN AND MOSS.

255 MOSS GROWS ON THE ROCKS FLANKING THE RIVER, CREATING AN ODD CHRISTMAS TREE.

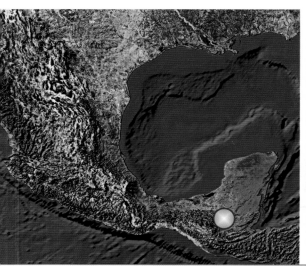

Reserva Cascadas de Agua Azul
Chiapas

The Chiapas region, in many ways rather dry and covered by vegetation composed of underbrush and succulents, contains some unique biological "islands" that have remained untouched by the economic development of the region because of their very limited accessibility. Many of these are found along the rivers, the ríos that en route to the ocean carve through plateaus and mountains, creating striking landscapes marked by deep canyons in the rocks.

In these canyons the vegetation of the arid zones turns into thick tropical cover maintained thanks to the humidity disseminated by the water. Trees, shrubs, lianas and epiphytes create a three-dimensional world in which most life forms flourishes well above ground level, taking advantage of the water that collects in the hollows of trees or at the base of bromeliads.

The Agua Azul Falls are among the most famous falls in all the world not only for the massive flow of water, which is of course affected by the amount of rainfall, nor for the impressive drop it flows over, but in the main for the biologic richness of the particular ecosystem of rainforest that grows near the falls.

The Reserva Cascadas de Agua Azull, extends over 152,826 acres (61,846 hectares), was established to protect the beauty of the landscape, to aid the conservation of the forest environments and water resources, and to promote tourist development in the area. Vegetation consists of pine and oak woods and xerophile ("aridity-loving") shrubbery in the upper part, and of acacia, alders and agaves in the lower part.

The fauna includes mammals such as wolves, deer and puma, although the presence of the last one is known from its tracks, not from direct observation. Snakes especially plentiful and includes boas, rattlesnakes, and liana snakes; avifauna includes toucans, quetzals, tanagers and multi-colored hummingbirds.

256 TOP THE TOUCAN IS A TYPICAL TROPICAL FOREST SPECIES, AND NUMEROUS MACAWS,.KNOWN FOR THEIR MULTICOLORED FEATHERS, POPULATE THE PROTECTED AREA.

256-257 RAPIDS AND WATERFALLS CHARACTERIZE A MAJOR PART OF THE RIVER'S COURSE.

257 THE AGUA AZIL FALLS ARE CHARACTERIZED BY UNPREDICTABLE FLOWS DURING THE SEASONS.

258-259 FLORA TYPICAL OF TROPICAL REGIONS GROWS DENSELY ALONG THE RIVER BANKS.

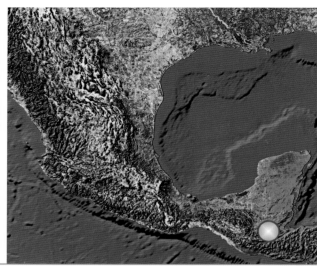

260 TOP LEFT THE BLACK HOWLER MONKEY EXHIBITS ITSELF IN A FANTASTIC CHORUS OF ROARS. GROUPS OF HOWLER MONKEYS USE THIS VOCAL ASSAULT TO WARN OTHERS TO STAY OFF THEIR TERRITORY.

260-261 AN ABUNDANT FLORA OF TREES, SHRUBS, TROPICAL VINES AND EPIPHYTES GROWS IN A LARGE PART OF THE PROTECTED AREA.

261 EVERY TRUNK IN THE FOREST REPRESENTS A MICRO-ECOSYSTEM FOR THE MULTITUDE OF EPIPHYTIC PLANTS WHICH IT HOSTS.

National Park of Tikal
Guatemala

This protected area, named a natural monument in 1931 and transformed into a national park in 1955, is located inside the Petén District, in northeastern Guatemala and is part of the immense Maya Biosphere Reserve, which extends over 10 percent of Guatemalan territory. In all the reserve encompasses 8100 sq. miles (21,000 sq. km).

In 1991, because of its value as a series of landscapes, its extraordinary geological constitution, its biological resources and its human population, the area earned inclusion in UNESCO's Man and Biosphere program. The Maya Biosphere Reserve constitutes, along with the Maya Forest in Belize and Mexico, one of the largest areas of tropical forest north of the Amazon, and in location it is the most northerly in the Western Hemisphere.

The area is composed of ancient rocks from the Mesozoic period, and more recent ones that date from the Tertiary period. They are of sedimentary origin and form small hills in the north and the Lacandon mountain range in the central zone.

The climate is warm and humid, with rainfall that exceeds 80 inches (200 cm) per year. Most of the district is covered by a lush tropical forest of almost 54,500 acres (22,000 hectares) with trees that reach the height of 130 feet (40 m) and with a complex community of lianas and epiphytes that climb up trunks and branches in a perennial struggle to reach the sunlight.

The forest at times gives way to vast humid zones, lagoons and *aguadas*, surface swamps rich with birdlife – ducks, herons, spoonbills, ibis, egrets and other species). These *aguadas* constitute one of the most important marsh systems in Central America.

Numerous rivers within the Usumacinta River basin flow through the park, en route to the Gulf of Mexico.

A preliminary inventory of the biodiversity within the area has identified more than 2000 plants and a several hundreds of species of vertebrates, among which are the jaguar, the armadillo, the otter, the puma and the tapir. Avifauna consists of more than 333 species of birds; in fact, 63 of the 74 avian families present in Guatemala are represented. Reptiles and amphibians include Morelet's crocodile, and 38 snake species.

The park also contains the remains of a once densely populated Mayan city, abandoned in about the 10th century, a fact that bears witness to the long distant transition of a hunting and gathering civilization to an agricultural one, now too passed away.

262 TOP A SCARLET MACAW, A SPECIES WHICH LIVES IN TROPICAL AND ECUADORIAN FORESTS. IT FEEDS ON NUTS AND OTHER FRUITS OF THE FOREST.

262 BOTTOM IN SOME PARTS OF THE FOREST, THE AMOUNT OF LIGHT THAT REACHES THE GROUND IS SO SCARCE THAT PROPER UNDERGROWTH IS UNABLE TO GROW.

263 THE JAGUAR LIVES MOSTLY IN THE LEAST ACCESSIBLE PARTS OF THE PROTECTED AREA, HUNTING WILD PIGS AND TAPIRS.

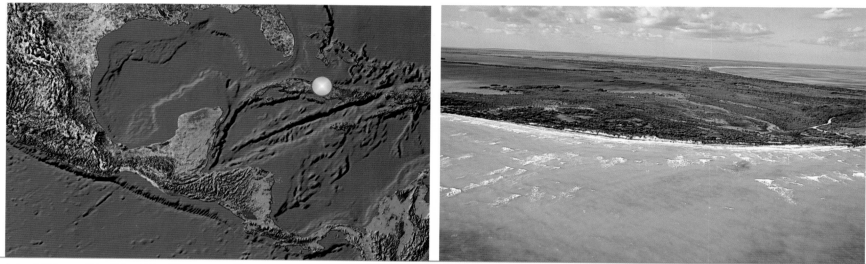

Cayo Coco
Cuba

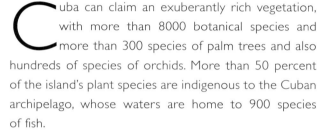

uba can claim an exuberantly rich vegetation, with more than 8000 botanical species and more than 300 species of palm trees and also hundreds of species of orchids. More than 50 percent of the island's plant species are indigenous to the Cuban archipelago, whose waters are home to 900 species of fish.

The Cayo Coco Reserve is dedicated specifically to the conservation of the marine ecosystem on and around Cayo Coco, the fourth largest island of the Cuban archipelago, 143 sq. miles (370 sq. km) in size, lying off Cuba's north shore, facing the Old Bahamas Channel.

It is a place that has become famous in recent years among undersea diving enthusiasts for the beauty of the seafloor and the clearness of the water.

Facing a 6-mile (9.5 km) long beach of superfine sand is a coral reef considered one of the richest on the planet; it rivals Australia's Great Barrier Reef and also the Red Sea Coral Reef. Thousands of species of marine invertebrates and multicolored fish gather among gorgonia and coral of every shape, color and size: soft and hard coral, antler coral, brain coral, lamina coral — the refuge of parrot fish and surgeonfish, butterfly fish and large groupers. Just beyond the coral reef, where the ocean floor drops rather steeply, the kingdom of the shark and other large-sized predators begins.

The district, which is open for the enjoyment of the public thanks to a series of diving and snorkeling practice centers, is surrounded by a dense tropical forest inhabited by multicolored hummingbirds and by many other species of birds. Also of particular interest is the coastal area, which is frequented by seabirds and flocks of flamingos that in some cases can number 30,000 or more.

The typical coastal vegetation of mangroves grows here, in one of Earth's most endangered habitats, of vital importance for the reproduction and growth of many forms of life, including the large tree-iguana.

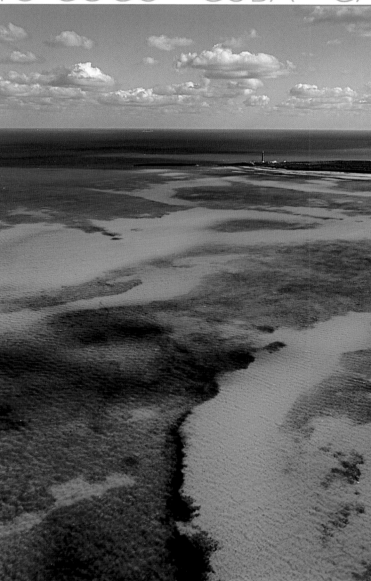

264 TOP RIGHT THE CORAL REEF IS CONSIDERED TO BE AMONG THE RICHEST OF THE PLANET, TO THE POINT THAT IT RIVALS BOTH THE AUSTRALIA'S GREAT BARRIER REEF AND THE RED SEA.

264-265 THE PROTECTED AREA OFFERS SAMPLE OF THE GREAT VARIETY OF FLORA FOUND IN THE IN CUBA, WHICH COUNTS OVER 8000 BOTANICAL SPECIES AND OVER 300 SPECIES OF PALMS.

265 THE PROTECTED AREA HAS BECOME FAMOUS IN THE PAST YEARS AMONG SCUBA DIVING ENTHUSIASTS FOR THE SPLENDOR OF ITS DEPTHS AND THE WATER.

266-267 IT IS ESTIMATED THAT THERE ARE THOUSANDS OF DIFFERENT SPECIES OF
MARINE INVERTEBRATES AND MULTI-COLORED FISH PRESENT IN THE BARRIER. THE
DOLPHIN IS ALSO A VERY COMMON SPECIES WHICH IS FOUND IN THE BAYS.

267 TOP CORAL FORMATIONS, UNDERWATER PRAIRIES AND SANDY DEPTHS ARE
A REFUGE FOR SEA TURTLES.

267 BOTTOM THE MARINI FAUNA FOUND IN THE CORAL REEF INCLUDES OF PARROT
AND SURGEON FISH, BUTTERFLY FISH AND LARGE GROUPERS.

INDEX - INDEX - INDEX - INDEX - INDEX - INDEX - INDEX - INDEX -

Page 134 David Muench/Corbis

Pages 134-135 Scott T. Smith/DanitaDelimont.com

Page 135 left John Shaw/NHPA/Photoshot

Page 135 right Galen Rowell/Corbis

Pages 136-137 David Muench/Corbis

Pages 138 left and right, 138-139,139 bottom and 140-141 Antonio Attini/Archivio White Star

Pages 142-143 Galen Rowell/Mountain Light

Pages 144-145 Antonio Attini/Archivio White Star

Pages 146 right, 146-147, 147 top and bottom, 148 top and bottom, 148-149 Jim Wark

Pages 150 top and bottom, 150-151 and 151 left and right Antonio Attini/Archivio White Star

Pages 186 left and right, 186-187 and 187 top and bottom Brandon Cole

Pages 188-189 Tim Davis/Corbis

Page 190 Douglas Peebles/Corbis

Pages 190-191 Alan Becker/Getty Images

Page 191 left Bill Heinsohn/Getty Images

Page 191 right NASA

Pages 192-193 Bryan Lowry/SeaPics.com

Page 193 top and bottom and 194-195 G. Brad Lewis/Getty Images

Pages 196 top and bottom, 196-197, 197 left and center, 198 top and bottom and 199 Antonio Attini/Archivio White Star

Page 200 top and bottom Altrendo Nature/Getty Images

Pages 234 top, center, bottom, 234-235 and 235 Antonio Attini/Archivio White Star

Pages 236 and 236-237 Jim Wark

Page 237 left Corbis

Page 238 left Charlotte & Parker Bauer

Page 238 top right David Muench/Corbis

Page 238 right center Tom Vezo/Naturepl.com/Contrasto

Page 238 bottom right Craig Lovell/Eagle Visions Photography/Alamy

Page 239 George H. H. Huey/Corbis

Page 240 Galen Rowell/Mountain Light

Pages 240-241 Mark Newman/Lonely Planet Images

Page 241 left Claudio Contreras

Page 152 right Jim Wark

Pages 152-153 Werner Bollmann/Agefotostock/Marka

Page 153 W. Perry Conway/Corbis

Pages 154-155 and 156-157 Jim Wark

Page 158 top Jim Wark

Page 158 bottom Antonio Attini/Archivio White Star

Pages 158-159 Jim Wark

Page 159 left Antonio Attini/Archivio White Star

Pages 160, 160-161,161 top and bottom and 162-163 Marcello Bertinetti/Archivio White Star

Pages 164 top Galen Rowell/Corbis

Page 164 bottom Ron Watts/Corbis

Pages 164-165 Galen Rowell/Mountain Light

Page 165 right Galen Rowell/Corbis

Page 166 Altrendo Nature/Getty Images

Page 167 top Fritz Poelking/Agefotostock/Marka

Page 167 center Randall Levensaler/Getty Images

Page 167 bottom Dewitt Jones/Corbis

Pages 168-169 Steve Satushek/Getty Images

Pages 170-171 Fred Hirschmann/Getty Images

Page 172 Jim Wark

Pages 172-173 Marcello Bertinetti/Archivio White Star

Page 173 left Eddie Brady/Lonely Planet Images

Pages 174-175 David Muench/Corbis

Page 175 Antonio Attini/Archivio White Star

Page 176 right Daniel J. Cox/Getty Images

Pages 176-177 Galen Rowell/Corbis

Page 177 Miles Ertman/Masterfile/Sie

Page 178 top left Marcello Bertinetti/Archivio White Star

Page 178 center Galen Rowell/Corbis

Page 179 Galen Rowell/Mountain Light

Pages 180-181 W. Perry Conway/Corbis

Page 182 right Nik Wheeler/Corbis

Pages 182-183 Stephen Saks/Lonely Planet Images

Pages 183 and 184 George H. H. Huey/Corbis

Page 185 top Rich Kirchner/NHPA/Photoshot

Page 185 center Roy Toft/Getty Images

Page 185 George H. H. Huey/Corbis

Pages 200-201 Louise Psihoyos/Corbis

Page 201 left Norbert Rosing/Getty Images

Page 201 right and 202 Antonio Attini/Archivio White Star

Pages 202-203 Witold Skrypczak/Lonely Planet Images

Pages 204-205 Jim Wark

Pages 206 and 206-207 Jim Wark

Page 207 left Antonio Attini/Archivio White Star

Page 208 Antonio Attini/Archivio White Star

Pages 208-209 Jim Wark

Page 209 top and bottom Antonio Attini/Archivio White Star

Pages 210-211 Tom Walker/Getty Images

Page 212 right Joh Cancalosi/Ardea.com

Pages 212-213 Antonio Attini/Archivio White Star

Page 213 Ingo Ardnt

Pages 214-215 R. Oggiorni/Panda Photo

Page 216 Steve Dunwell/Agefotostock/Marka

Pages 216-217 Jim Wark

Page 217 left Swerve/Alamy

Page 218 top Kim Grant/Lonely Planet Images

Page 218 bottom Peter Arnold Inc./Alamy

Pages 218-219 D. Robert & Lorri Franz/Corbis

Pages 220 and 220-221 Cameron Davidson/Alamy

Page 221 right Lynda Richardson/Corbis

Pages 222-223 Thad Samuels Abell II/Getty Images

Page 224 right Buddy Mays/Corbis

Pages 224-225 Adam Jones/DanitaDelimont.com

Page 225 top Tom Breakefield/Corbis

Page 225 bottom Adam Jones/DanitaDelimont.com

Pages 226-227 Joanne Wells/DanitaDelimont.com

Pages 228-229 Pat O' Hara/Corbis

Page 229 top Alan & Sandy Carey/zefa/Corbis

Page 229 bottom Adam Jones/DanitaDelimont.com

Page 230 top Daniel J. Cox/Natural Exposure.com

Page 230 bottom Marcello Bertinetti/Archivio White Star

Pages 230-231 Antonio Attini/Archivio White Star

Page 231 right Jim Wark

Pages 232 top and bottom, 232-233 and 233 left and right Marcello Bertinetti/Archivio White Star

Page 242 right David & Irene Myers/NHPA/Photoshot

Page 242 Claudio Contreras

Pages 242-243 Heeb/Agefotostock/Marka

Page 243 left Claudio Contreras

Page 244 Jim Wark

Page 245 top Francois Gohier/Auscape

Page 245 bottom Doug Perrine/Naturepl.com/Contrasto

Page 246 right Claudio Contreras

Pages 246-247 Andoni Canela/Agefotostock/Marka

Page 247 Andy Rouse/Getty Images

Pages 248-249 Antonio Attini/Archivio White Star

Page 250 and 250-251 Claudio Contreras

Page 251 top Michele Westmorland/DanitaDelimont.com

Page 251 bottom Claudio Contreras

Pages 252 right and 252-253 Antonio Attini/Archivio White Star

Page 253 Adalberto Rios/Agefotostock/Marka

Pages 254-255 John Mitchell

Page 255 Charles Crust/DanitaDelimont.com

Page 256 center P. Lavoretti/Panda Photo

Page 256 right Stephen Dalton/NHPA/Photoshot

Pages 256-257 Massimo Borchi/Archivio White Star

Page 257 Jon Arnold/DanitaDelimont.com

Pages 258-259 Claudio Contreras

Page 260 left Tim Laman/Getty Images

Pages 260-261, 261 and 262 top Craig Lovell/Eagle Visions Photography

Page 262 bottom Andoni Canela/Agefotostock/Marka

Page 263 Charlotte & Parker Bauer

Pages 264 right, 264-265 and 265 Antonio Attini/Archivio White Star

Pages 266-267 and 267 top Doug Perrine Naturepl.com/Contrasto

Page 267 bottom Martino Fagiuoli

Page 272 Antonio Attini/Archivio White Star

Satellite maps by World Sat

272 THE ARCHES NATIONAL PARK, IN THE SOUTH-WEST OF UTAH,
BOASTS AN INCREDIBLE CONCENTRATION OF STONE NATURAL ARCHES.